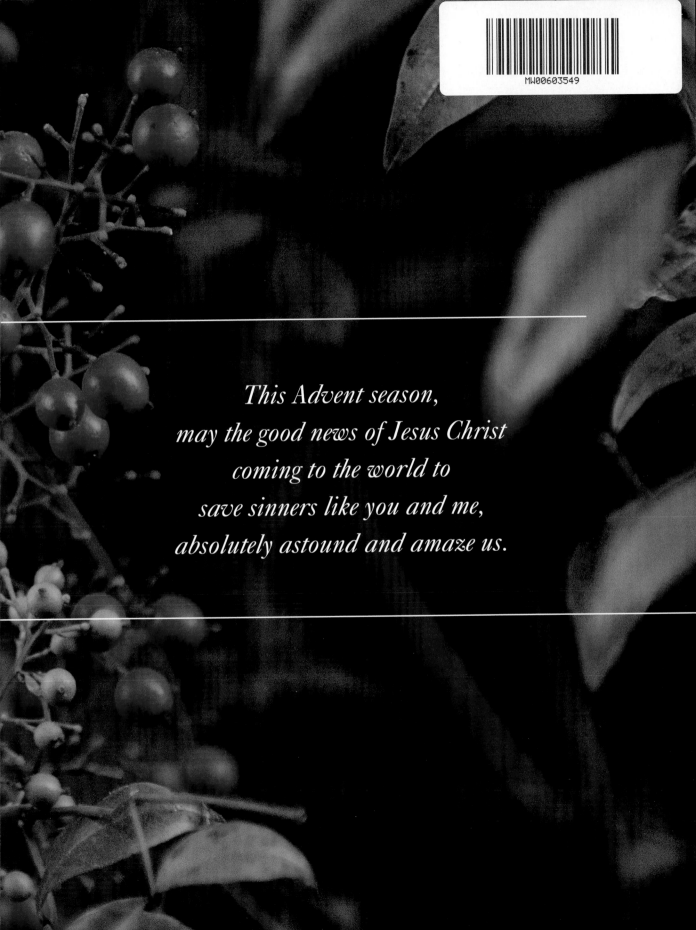

This Advent season,
may the good news of Jesus Christ
coming to the world to
save sinners like you and me,
absolutely astound and amaze us.

STUDY CONTRIBUTORS

Contributors:
STEFANIE BOYLES
AUBREY COLEMAN
JOANNA KIMBREL
KRISTYN PEREZ
KRISTIN SCHMUCKER
JANA WHITE

Designer:
KATIE LINSTRUM

Editor:
JANA WHITE

www.thedailygraceco.com

Designed in the United States of America and printed in China.

Hymns

FOR

Advent

TABLE
OF
CONTENTS

WEEK ONE
DAY ONE

CANDLE LIGHTING DAY

The Hope Candle

A candle is lit on each Sunday of Advent in many churches and homes that follow the church calendar. On the first Sunday of Advent, the candle symbolizes hope. The entire Advent season is a season of hope and of waiting and anticipation for the Messiah. But biblical hope is not just wishful thinking; it is hopeful expectation. It is absolute certainty. So as we are reminded of the hope of the coming Messiah, we can also be reminded of the assurance of salvation for all who are united to Christ. The promises of God are steadfast and sure and we can have full confidence that God will do what He has said He will do. We place our hope in Jesus because He is our hope.

1 PETER 1:3

Blessed be the God and Father of our Lord Jesus Christ. Because of his great mercy he has given us new birth into a living hope through the resurrection of Jesus Christ from the dead

IT CAME UPON A MIDNIGHT CLEAR,
THAT GLORIOUS SONG OF OLD,
FROM ANGELS BENDING NEAR
THE EARTH TO TOUCH THEIR
HARPS OF GOLD:
"PEACE ON THE EARTH, GOOD WILL
TO MEN, FROM HEAVEN'S ALL-
GRACIOUS KING."
THE WORLD IN SOLEMN STILLNESS
LAY, TO HEAR THE ANGELS SING.

STILL THROUGH THE CLOVEN
SKIES THEY COME WITH PEACEFUL
WINGS UNFURLED, AND STILL THEIR
HEAVENLY MUSIC FLOATS O'ER ALL
THE WEARY WORLD;
ABOVE ITS SAD AND LOWLY PLAINS,
THEY BEND ON HOVERING WING,
AND EVER O'ER ITS BABEL SOUNDS
THE BLESSED ANGELS SING.

AND YE, BENEATH LIFE'S
CRUSHING LOAD, WHOSE FORMS
ARE BENDING LOW, WHO TOIL
ALONG THE CLIMBING WAY WITH
PAINFUL STEPS AND SLOW, LOOK
NOW! FOR GLAD AND GOLDEN
HOURS COME SWIFTLY ON THE
WING. O REST BESIDE THE WEARY
ROAD, AND HEAR THE ANGELS SING!

FOR LO! THE DAYS ARE HASTENING
ON, BY PROPHET SEEN OF OLD,
WHEN WITH THE EVER-CIRCLING
YEARS SHALL COME THE TIME
FORETOLD: WHEN PEACE SHALL
OVER ALL THE EARTH ITS ANCIENT
SPLENDORS FLING, AND THE WHOLE
WORLD SEND BACK THE SONG
WHICH NOW THE ANGELS SING.

It Came UPON A *Midnight Clear*

———

The word advent means coming or arrival. The season of Advent is a time to prepare our hearts for the coming of our Savior, Jesus Christ. In the weeks leading up to Christmas, we want to experience the longing as God's people did as they waited eagerly for the arrival of the One whom the prophets foretold. And even though He came to earth as a human more than 2,000 years ago, we still await a second Advent. We wait for the day when Christ will return once again and consummate the Kingdom that He has inaugurated, restoring what was destroyed by sin and making all things new in the presence of God.

Music has a unique ability to captivate our imaginations, steer our affections, and express the intricacies of our emotions. Music is a beautiful gift from God that has been used throughout human history to rejoice in the works and character of God, to lament the brokenness caused by sin, and to encourage one another with the gospel. Throughout this study, it is our goal to cultivate our longing for Christ through Christmas hymns written over thousands of years, all of which point to the hope of Jesus Christ.

As we begin our study with a well-known Christmas hymn, "It Came Upon a Midnight Clear," we look back to the night when the angels announced the good news of Jesus' birth to the shepherds. The announcement of this birth was not just the news of a child, but of the coming of the promised Messiah, the Anointed One whom the prophets and all of Scripture foretold. This child was promised as early as the third chapter in Genesis when the sin of man first came into play. God created the world and called it good, but Adam and Eve disobeyed, introducing sin to human nature along with its devastating consequence — death. Even as God pronounced the curse upon man, He made a promise. He promised that a redeemer would come from the seed of the woman, one who would crush the head of the deceiver and bring God's people back to Himself. The hope and promise of this offspring run throughout all of Scripture, and on that night in Bethlehem, all of those promises find fulfillment in Jesus Christ.

The song paints a picture of a solemn darkness interrupted by a glorious refrain. When Christ was born, He entered into a world weary with sin and waiting in darkness for the One who would bring the light of salvation. God's people had experienced slavery, destruction, and exile. And while they clung to the promises of God delivered through His prophets, it seemed as if God had gone silent. Then, in the dark midnight of their waiting, in God's perfect timing, Christ appeared.

The world is still filled with the darkness of sin, but the light of the gospel shimmers in anticipation of the everlasting light that will banish all darkness. Our weak frames may bend beneath the crushing load of life, but the hope of the gospel lifts our burdens and places them on Christ. We may feel as if the journey of this life is long, slow, and painful, but this Advent season calls us to look to the golden hours that break through the gloom of night. As we prepare our hearts for Christmas, let us "rest beside the weary road and hear the angels sing," and may our hearts join in their joyous melody!

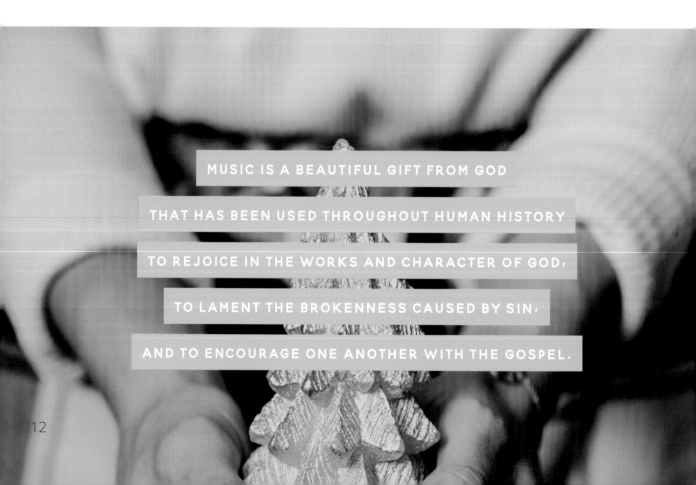

MUSIC IS A BEAUTIFUL GIFT FROM GOD

THAT HAS BEEN USED THROUGHOUT HUMAN HISTORY

TO REJOICE IN THE WORKS AND CHARACTER OF GOD,

TO LAMENT THE BROKENNESS CAUSED BY SIN,

AND TO ENCOURAGE ONE ANOTHER WITH THE GOSPEL.

THROUGH THIS HYMN WE ARE REMINDED THAT THE GOSPEL POINTS US TOWARDS
THE EVERLASTING LIGHT, JESUS CHRIST, WHO WILL BANISH ALL DARKNESS.
HOW DOES THIS BRING HOPE TO OUR DARKER DAYS?

WHAT OTHER TRUTHS DO YOU DRAW FROM THIS HYMN AND HOW DO THEY STIR
YOUR AFFECTIONS FOR CHRIST?

WRITE A PRAYER OF PREPARATION FOR THE COMING ADVENT SEASON, INVITING GOD
TO PREPARE YOUR HEART AS YOU ARE REMINDED OF THE BEAUTIFUL TRUTHS FOUND
IN THIS STUDY OF CHRISTMAS HYMNS.

O COME, O COME, EMMANUEL, AND RANSOM CAPTIVE ISRAEL THAT MOURNS IN LONELY EXILE HERE UNTIL THE SON OF GOD APPEAR.

REJOICE! REJOICE! EMMANUEL SHALL COME TO YOU, O ISRAEL.

O COME, O WISDOM FROM ON HIGH, WHO ORDERED ALL THINGS MIGHTILY; TO US THE PATH OF KNOWLEDGE SHOW AND TEACH US IN ITS WAYS TO GO.

O COME, O COME, GREAT LORD OF MIGHT, WHO TO YOUR TRIBES ON SINAI'S HEIGHT IN ANCIENT TIMES DID GIVE THE LAW IN CLOUD AND MAJESTY AND AWE.

O COME, O BRANCH OF JESSE'S STEM, UNTO YOUR OWN AND RESCUE THEM! FROM DEPTHS OF HELL YOUR PEOPLE SAVE, AND GIVE THEM VICTORY O'ER THE GRAVE.

O COME, O KEY OF DAVID, COME AND OPEN WIDE OUR HEAVENLY HOME. MAKE SAFE FOR US THE HEAVENWARD ROAD AND BAR THE WAY TO DEATH'S ABODE.

O COME, O BRIGHT AND MORNING STAR, AND BRING US COMFORT FROM AFAR! DISPEL THE SHADOWS OF THE NIGHT AND TURN OUR DARKNESS INTO LIGHT.

O COME, O KING OF NATIONS, BIND IN ONE THE HEARTS OF ALL MANKIND. BID ALL OUR SAD DIVISIONS CEASE AND BE YOURSELF OUR KING OF PEACE.

O Come, O COME, Emmanuel

The well-known Christmas hymn, "O Come, O Come, Emmanuel," is a song that has been sung for hundreds of years. It is a cry of longing for Jesus, the Savior promised throughout the pages of Scripture. Each verse of the hymn contains a different messianic name found in Scriptures that point to the promised Messiah. The verses of this hymn invite us to look both back to the first coming of Christ that the people of God in the Old Testament waited for, and forward to His second coming. During the Advent season, we celebrate His first coming, but we also long for the day when He will return again and make everything right.

God is Emmanuel, which means "God with us." God's plan has always been to dwell with His people as He did with Adam and Eve in the beginning. But because of their sin, He sent them away from His manifest presence, but God did not abandon His original design. Before He sent them away, He made a promise of a savior. And in Isaiah 7:14 we read that a virgin would bear a son named Emmanuel. This would be the Savior. And hundreds of years later, that child was born. Jesus was literally God Himself dwelling among us, and by His sacrifice on the cross, He made a way for our sins to be covered that we might draw near to the holy God. All who have faith in Him have the Holy Spirit of God dwelling in us, and we await the day when Christ will come again and bring down the dwelling place of God to be with man at last. During Advent, we rejoice that Christ came down to be God with us, and we long for the day when we will experience the uninhibited, manifest presence of the Lord.

Jesus is also the Rod of Jesse, which is a reference to Isaiah 11:1-2. Jesse was the father of King David, and God made a promise to David that the Messiah would come from His line and rule on an everlasting throne, but in 586 B.C. the kingdom of Judah was exiled by the Babylonians and the line of Davidic kings was cut off. It seemed as if God's promises had failed, but He said that a shoot, or a rod, would spring up out of the stump of Jesse. Jesus Christ is the Son of David, life springing up from what appeared to be dead, ruling on the throne as the true King and Lord of all. Jesus inaugurated His Kingdom here on earth, and one day He will return to consummate it. He will rule over all of creation in righteousness and peace, and every tongue will confess His lordship.

Dayspring is another title given to Jesus in this hymn. This word carries the meaning of sunrise or dawn. Zechariah, the father of John the Baptist, referred to the coming Messiah using this name when he prophesied about Jesus in Luke 1:78. Jesus is the sunrise after the night that brings hope to the nations. Jesus is the light of the world that breaks through the darkness. Jesus fulfills the words of the prophecy in Isaiah 9:2 when it says, "The people walking in darkness have seen a great light; on those living in the land of darkness, a light has dawned." This metaphor of Jesus being the light and hope to the darkness of sin and death runs throughout Scripture. The light has come, and now we look forward to the day when it will totally push out the darkness. Jesus calls Himself the bright morning star in Revelation 22:16, and we long for the day when His glory among us shines brighter than the sun or moon or stars (Revelation 21:23).

As we sing this song, we rejoice in the truth that the Messiah has come, bringing with Him hope and joy and peace. We also are keenly aware of the fact that we still live in a fallen world, and although Jesus Christ has inaugurated His Kingdom, we still await its consummation. God was faithful to bring about the Messiah, just as He promised, and He will be faithful to fulfill every promise. And so we allow the promises of God to stir in our hearts a desire for a day when every single one will be completely fulfilled in Jesus Christ.

JESUS WAS LITERALLY GOD HIMSELF DWELLING AMONG US, AND BY HIS SACRIFICE ON THE CROSS, HE MADE A WAY FOR OUR SINS TO BE COVERED THAT WE MIGHT DRAW NEAR TO THE HOLY GOD.

HOW DOES UNDERSTANDING THE MESSIANIC NAMES ENRICH YOUR EXPERIENCE
OF THIS FAMILIAR SONG?

WHICH MESSIANIC NAME STIRS THE GREATEST LONGING IN YOU FOR
JESUS' SECOND COMING AND WHY?

HOW DOES THE MESSAGE OF "O COME, O COME EMMANUEL" GIVE YOU HOPE
AS YOU LIVE IN THIS FALLEN WORLD?

O HOLY NIGHT, THE STARS ARE
BRIGHTLY SHINING, IT IS THE NIGHT
OF THE DEAR SAVIOUR'S BIRTH;
LONG LAY THE WORLD IN SIN AND
ERROR PINING, 'TILL HE APPEARED
AND THE SOUL FELT ITS WORTH.
A THRILL OF HOPE THE WEARY
WORLD REJOICES,
FOR YONDER BREAKS A NEW
AND GLORIOUS MORN;

FALL ON YOUR KNEES, OH HEAR
THE ANGEL VOICES! O NIGHT DIVINE!
O NIGHT WHEN CHRIST WAS BORN.
O NIGHT, O HOLY NIGHT,
O NIGHT DIVINE.

LED BY THE LIGHT OF FAITH
SERENELY BEAMING; WITH GLOWING
HEARTS BY HIS CRADLE WE STAND:
SO, LED BY LIGHT OF A STAR
SWEETLY GLEAMING, HERE COME
THE WISE MEN FROM ORIENT LAND,
THE KING OF KINGS LAY THUS IN
LOWLY MANGER, IN ALL OUR TRIALS
BORN TO BE OUR FRIEND;

HE KNOWS OUR NEED, TO OUR
WEAKNESS NO STRANGER!
BEHOLD YOUR KING! BEFORE HIM
LOWLY BEND! BEHOLD YOUR KING!
YOUR KING! BEFORE HIM BEND!

TRULY HE TAUGHT US TO LOVE ONE
ANOTHER; HIS LAW IS LOVE AND HIS
GOSPEL IS PEACE; CHAINS SHALL
HE BREAK, FOR THE SLAVE IS OUR
BROTHER, AND IN HIS NAME ALL
OPPRESSION SHALL CEASE,
SWEET HYMNS OF JOY IN GRATEFUL
CHORUS RAISE WE; LET ALL WITHIN
US PRAISE HIS HOLY NAME!

CHRIST IS THE LORD, THEN EVER!
EVER PRAISE WE! HIS POW'R AND
GLORY, EVERMORE PROCLAIM!
HIS POW'R AND GLORY, EVERMORE
PROCLAIM!

O Holy Night

We may pass over the words of this song with ease and memorization, but the words we sing tell us something. These lyrics hold profound gospel truths. Three simple words announcing the birth of Christ to the world reveal the theme of this age-old hymn, "O Holy Night." The lyrics follow the rhythm of Luke chapter two, telling the story of the birth of Jesus, followed by the announcement of the angels, the wise men who followed the star, and the resounding hope this news would bring to all of the world.

One stanza stands out for its beautifully articulated
representation of the gospel:

Long lay the world
In sin and error pining,
Till He appeared
And the soul felt its worth.

The implication at the beginning of this line portrays a world that waits in longing. This is precisely what we read about in God's Word. Every part of creation was disordered and searching for restoration. In their longing, they continued their search in sin and error pining. Because of sin's record to over promise and under deliver, the world waited in hope for a savior, a king. Creation longed for the One who could redeem our brokenness and make all things new (Romans 8:22).

The hope of the Advent season is that God did not abandon us or leave us to ourselves. He loved us enough to make a way to restore what was broken and to fulfill the longings of our hearts. He promised a Savior would be born to us as a child. He appeared! And when He appeared, the world would never be the same. The coming of Jesus Christ was the answer to our longings and our hope for redemption. The Savior, Jesus the King, would be born in a stable on that holy night in Bethlehem. In His infancy, He would hold the hope of the world.

This hymn sings of the culmination of the appearance of Jesus Christ, and the soul felt its worth. Since the fall, the world has been left searching for anything that could satisfy the longing of our souls. Whether relationships or families, success and accomplishments, wealth and fortune, health and long lives, these are all pursuits born out of a longing for worth and purpose. It is undeniable that we cannot find it in and of ourselves. But God directs us to where our souls are satisfied. The psalmist writes, "For it was you who created my inward parts; you knit me together in my mother's womb. I will praise you because I have been remarkably and wondrously made. Your works are wondrous and I know this very well" (Psalm 139:13-14). At the core of our being, we long to be reunited with our Maker. We long to belong to the One who formed us and knitted us together.

What a holy night! The coming of Christ means that souls can find their worth in the hope of Jesus, and so we rejoice. For in this hope we have been saved and given a glimpse of a new day, a glorious morn. God has fulfilled His promise to us by sending Jesus. He promises that Christ will come again and unite all of His people together under His reign and rule. Romans 8:23 points us towards this future glory, "Not only that, but we ourselves who have the Spirit as the firstfruits—we also groan within ourselves, eagerly waiting for adoption, the redemption of our bodies." This is true and lasting worth of the soul and it is found in Jesus Christ alone. God made us for Himself, and our souls are stirring until they find their place in Him.

THE HOPE OF THE ADVENT SEASON IS THAT

GOD DID NOT ABANDON US OR LEAVE US TO OURSELVES.

HE LOVED US ENOUGH TO MAKE A WAY TO RESTORE WHAT WAS

BROKEN AND TO FULFILL THE LONGINGS OF OUR HEARTS.

HOW DOES ROMANS 3:10-18 DESCRIBE HOW THE WORLD LAYS IN "SIN AND ERROR"
AS A RESULT OF THE CURSE OF SIN THAT TOOK PLACE IN GENESIS?

PINING MEANS TO WAIT IN LONGING. IN ROMANS 8:22-25 WE SEE THE TERM GROANING.
WHAT SIMILARITIES DO YOU FIND IN THE MEANING OF THESE TWO TERMS?
HOW DOES THIS PASSAGE EXPLAIN THE IDEA THAT THE WORLD IS PINING FOR A SAVIOR?

WHAT DOES IT MEAN THAT WE FIND OUR TRUE WORTH IN JESUS CHRIST?
HOW DOES THIS TRUTH ENCOURAGE YOU TODAY?

ONCE IN ROYAL DAVID'S CITY
STOOD A LOWLY CATTLE SHED,
WHERE A MOTHER LAID HER BABY
IN A MANGER FOR HIS BED:
MARY WAS THAT MOTHER MILD,
JESUS CHRIST HER LITTLE CHILD.

HE CAME DOWN TO EARTH FROM
HEAVEN, WHO IS GOD AND LORD
OF ALL, AND HIS SHELTER WAS
A STABLE, AND HIS CRADLE WAS
A STALL; WITH THE POOR, AND
MEAN, AND LOWLY, LIVED ON
EARTH OUR SAVIOR HOLY.

AND THROUGH ALL HIS WONDROUS
CHILDHOOD HE WOULD HONOR
AND OBEY, LOVE AND WATCH THE
LOWLY MAIDEN, IN WHOSE GENTLE
ARMS HE LAY: CHRISTIAN CHILDREN
ALL MUST BE MILD, OBEDIENT,
GOOD AS HE.

FOR HE IS OUR CHILDHOOD'S
PATTERN; DAY BY DAY, LIKE US
HE GREW; HE WAS LITTLE, WEAK
AND HELPLESS, TEARS AND
SMILES LIKE US HE KNEW; AND HE
FEELETH FOR OUR SADNESS, AND
HE SHARETH IN OUR GLADNESS.

AND OUR EYES AT LAST SHALL SEE
HIM, THROUGH HIS OWN REDEEMING
LOVE; FOR THAT CHILD SO DEAR
AND GENTLE IS OUR LORD IN
HEAVEN ABOVE, AND HE LEADS
HIS CHILDREN ON TO THE PLACE
WHERE HE IS GONE.

NOT IN THAT POOR LOWLY STABLE,
WITH THE OXEN STANDING BY, WE
SHALL SEE HIM; BUT IN HEAVEN,
SET AT GOD'S RIGHT HAND ON HIGH;
WHERE LIKE STARS HIS CHILDREN
CROWNED ALL IN WHITE SHALL
WAIT AROUND.

Read: Philippians 2:5-11, Hebrews 2:14-18

Once in Royal David's City

The nativity scene is a familiar sight during the Christmas season. The images of baby Jesus lying in a manger, surrounded by animals and hay, as Mary, Joseph, shepherds, and wisemen look reverently at the child, adorn our homes, our neighbors' front yards, our churches, and Christmas cards we receive in the mail. The picture of the Christ child in the cattle shed may seem ordinary to us, but its implications are absolutely extraordinary. The Christmas hymn, "Once in Royal David's City," beautifully illustrates the truth that God in His incredible grace came down to sinners in order to save them.

The baby born to Mary on that night was not an ordinary child, but the Son of God Himself. Jesus Christ is the second person of the Trinity, fully divine and deserving of all glory and praise. But instead of tightening His grip on His own honor, He willingly gave it up and humbled Himself to become like us. The almighty Son of God, He "who is God and Lord of all," stooped low to become a helpless infant, born not in a palace that His royalty merits, but in a "lowly cattle shed." He was not even given the dignity of a bed, but He laid His head in an animals' feeding trough. The dirty barn in Bethlehem was just the beginning of the lowly existence to which Jesus, the Lord of the universe, willingly submitted Himself.

Jesus lived a life marked by the same difficulties that we experience. He took on human weakness and pain, and He can empathize with every kind of temptation and suffering that we endure. Instead of receiving His due honor wherever He went, Jesus was rejected and despised. The people He came to save gave Him a death sentence, and the perfect and sinless Christ was shamed as a criminal as He suffered an excruciating death on the cross. From His lowly birth all the way to His shameful death, Jesus willingly subjected Himself to all of it. Jesus came down to our level.

Jesus became like us in order to save us. Apart from Christ, we all have the same death sentence that He endured. We are all sinners deserving of the wrath of God, and the just penalty for our sin is death. Try as we might, there is nothing we can do, no amount of good works or religious activity, to climb our way into God's favor. Apart from Christ, we are hopeless, but rather than leave us in our sin, God loved us so much that He gave Himself for us. We could never ascend to God so God descended to us. The Son of God became a human, "little, weak, and helpless," and endured the pains of this life without ever sinning. He lived the righteous life that we could never live and traded His life for ours. He had to become like us, fully human, in order to pay the debt of death that we owed. The beauty of Christmas is not just that a child is born, but that the One who is high above the heavens came down to earth to suffer and die for us.

God's story does not end in pain, but in glory. After three days in the grave, God raised Jesus to life in victory over sin and death, and through faith in Him by the grace of God, we can have the life Christ earned through His righteousness. Christ ascended into heaven, and one day, as the hymn proclaims, we will see Him. He will come again and glorify us. The hope of "Once in Royal David's City" is the hope of the gospel: Jesus came down to us in order to raise us up with Him.

WE COULD NEVER ASCEND TO GOD

SO GOD DESCENDED TO US.

WHAT DOES CHRIST HUMBLING HIMSELF REVEAL ABOUT GOD'S CHARACTER?

WHAT DOES CHRIST HUMBLING HIMSELF REVEAL ABOUT OUR HUMAN NATURE?

GOD CAME DOWN TO US BECAUSE WE COULD NEVER REACH UP TO HIM.
HOW DO YOU SEE THE TENDENCY TO TRY TO ASCEND TO GOD IN YOUR OWN LIFE
INSTEAD OF ACCEPTING HIS CONDESCENDING GRACE?

COME, THOU LONG EXPECTED JESUS,
BORN TO SET THY PEOPLE FREE;
FROM OUR FEARS AND SINS
RELEASE US, LET US FIND OUR
REST IN THEE. ISRAEL'S STRENGTH
AND CONSOLATION, HOPE OF ALL
THE EARTH THOU ART; DEAR DESIRE
OF EVERY NATION, JOY OF EVERY
LONGING HEART.

BORN THY PEOPLE TO DELIVER,
BORN A CHILD AND YET A KING,
BORN TO REIGN IN US FOREVER,
NOW THY GRACIOUS KINGDOM
BRING. BY THINE OWN ETERNAL
SPIRIT RULE IN ALL OUR HEARTS
ALONE; BY THINE ALL SUFFICIENT
MERIT, RAISE US TO THY
GLORIOUS THRONE.

Read: Luke 2:23-35, Isaiah 42:1-3, Matthew 12:17-21, Titus 2:11

Come Thou
LONG
EXPECTED Jesus

Jesus is the long-expected One. In Genesis 3:15, there is the promise of One who would come even in the midst of the entrance of sin and separation from God. There was hope. Throughout the Old Testament Scriptures, there are promises that look forward to one—a better deliverer, a better king, a better prophet—the Messiah. But time and time again, generations would come and go—deliverers, rulers, kings, and prophets—but not one of them was the One who would bring salvation to the people. Yet still, there were some who looked forward to the coming of this promised Savior.

In Luke 2:23-35 we read about a man in Jerusalem whose name was Simeon. Scripture tells us that he was righteous and devout. He was looking forward to Israel's consolation—Israel's deliverance—and it had been revealed to him that he would not die before he saw the promised Messiah. Simeon is a representative of a remnant of Israel who had awaited the Messiah. He longed for the Messiah. But he did not long to see the Messiah without hope. The Holy Spirit had revealed to Simeon that he wouldn't see death before he saw the Messiah. So he waited, trusting in the promises of God. He exercised faith in what was to come.

Scripture tells us that Simeon entered the temple as he was guided by the Spirit. We don't have all the details of this interaction, but he took the baby Messiah in his arms and praised God. We do not know how he knew, but he did. And he rejoiced. It brought great joy to his soul when He held the baby, the Messiah, in his arms. He knew that this baby he was holding was the Messiah, the promised One of Israel, the One he had waited for.

Many of us would have likely questioned the appearance of this Messiah. How would a baby from common people be the Messiah of the world? He was neither clothed in royal linens, nor did He come from wealth. Yet, Simeon did not ask questions. He did not question the entrance of the baby, His family, or His majesty (or lack of). He had faith in the

Spirit's leading and knew that this was Him—the One he had waited for. He trusted in the promise of God and rested in that, regardless of whether the One matched the world's standards of a Messiah. This baby—Jesus—would be the consolation of Israel. He has come to save His people.

He is our consolation. The Messiah has come not just so that the Israelites would rejoice in their day, but that we could be beneficiaries also in the promise of salvation. Jesus the Messiah has come to save us from our sins with His own life. And in doing so, He has provided for our deepest need. The cry of our hearts should be for Him to come into our lives, bring salvation to our souls, and heal us. He is the perfect One who delivers us from our fears and our sins. In that truth we rest, we have hope, and we have joy.

Just as Simeon awaited the first coming of the Messiah, so we now as believers, await His second coming. We await His coming with anticipation. All of our deepest longings and devotion should reflect that of Simeon's as we look forward to the day when the Messiah will raise us with Him to His glorious throne. May we orient our hearts this season to the hope of Israel, the hope of those who have placed their faith in the risen Messiah who will return again in power to reign.

JESUS THE MESSIAH HAS COME TO SAVE US FROM OUR SINS WITH HIS OWN LIFE. AND IN DOING SO, HE HAS PROVIDED FOR OUR DEEPEST NEED.

SIMEON DESIRED TO SEE THE MESSIAH. DO WE LONG FOR JESUS AS SIMEON DID?
IF YOU NEED TO, SPEND TIME CONFESSING YOUR LACK OF DESIRE AND ASK THE SPIRIT
TO CULTIVATE A DESIRE FOR THE LORD JESUS IN YOUR HEART.

WHAT WOULD IT LOOK LIKE TO LOOK FORWARD TO THE SECOND COMING OF CHRIST AS
SIMEON AWAITED THE FIRST COMING OF CHRIST WITH ANTICIPATION?

WRITE A PRAYER PRAISING GOD THAT JESUS, THE ONE WHO SETS HIS PEOPLE FREE, HAS COME!

Week One Reflection

PARAPHRASE THE PASSAGES FROM THIS WEEK.

_____

_____

_____

_____

_____

_____

WHAT DID YOU OBSERVE FROM THIS WEEK'S TEXT ABOUT GOD AND HIS CHARACTER?

_____

_____

_____

_____

_____

_____

WHAT DO THESE PASSAGES TEACH ABOUT THE CONDITION OF MANKIND AND ABOUT YOURSELF?

_____

_____

_____

_____

_____

HOW DO THESE PASSAGES POINT TO THE GOSPEL?

_____

_____

_____

_____

_____

_____

HOW SHOULD YOU RESPOND TO THESE PASSAGES?
WHAT IS THE PERSONAL APPLICATION?

_____

_____

_____

_____

_____

_____

WHAT SPECIFIC ACTION STEPS CAN YOU TAKE THIS WEEK TO
APPLY THESE PASSAGES?

_____

_____

_____

_____

_____

_____

WEEK TWO
DAY ONE

CANDLE LIGHTING DAY

The Peace Candle

For the second week of Advent a candle is lit to symbolize peace and make our hearts yearn for Jesus who is the Prince of Peace (Isaiah 9:6). This peace is dependent fully on God and is not swayed by our circumstances. It is wholeness and completeness that is found in God alone. We have peace with God because Jesus has made peace in our place. This is not found in the absence of war or conflict, but it is found in the presence of Jesus. Jesus comes to make peace and to be our peace. And true peace is found only in Him.

PSALM 29:11

The Lord gives his people strength; the Lord blesses his people with peace.

LO, HOW A ROSE E'ER BLOOMING
FROM TENDER STEM HATH SPRUNG!
OF JESSE'S LINEAGE COMING
AS MEN OF OLD HAVE SUNG.
IT CAME, A FLOWER BRIGHT,
AMID THE COLD OF WINTER
WHEN HALF-GONE WAS THE NIGHT.

ISAIAH 'TWAS FORETOLD IT,
THE ROSE I HAVE IN MIND:
WITH MARY WE BEHOLD IT,
THE VIRGIN MOTHER KIND.
TO SHOW GOD'S LOVE ARIGHT
SHE BORE TO MEN A SAVIOR
WHEN HALF-GONE WAS THE NIGHT.

THIS FLOWER, WHOSE FRAGRANCE
TENDER WITH SWEETNESS FILLS
THE AIR, DISPELS WITH GLORIOUS
SPLENDOR THE DARKNESS
EVERYWHERE. TRUE MAN, YET
VERY GOD, FROM SIN AND DEATH
HE SAVES US AND LIGHTENS
EVERY LOAD.

Lo, How A ROSE E'er Blooming

"Lo How a Rose E'er Blooming" presents Jesus Christ as a flower that blooms in the dead of night and the cold of winter. It is a song of unimaginable hope in the midst of hope-lessness. It is a celebration of the faithfulness of God when it seems He has forgotten His promises. It heralds the good news of light in the darkness, beauty in brokenness, and life that springs forth from death.

The first verse describes a time of pain and waiting using the imagery of the cold of winter and the darkness of the middle of the night. When all seemed lost, a bright rose sprung forth amid the ice and darkness. The song describes this rose as coming from the lineage of Jesse. Jesse was the father of King David, from whose line God promised would come the promised Messiah, Jesus Christ, who would rule eternally as King. When the Southern Kingdom of Judah was exiled and the line of Davidic kings cut off, it seemed as if God had abandoned the promise of a Messiah King, but He promised One would come forth from Jesse's line, like a fresh shoot springing forth from a tree stump. The people waited and centuries passed without a new king to sit on David's throne, and for 430 years, God's people did not hear His voice. But then, in the wintry darkness of night, Jesus Christ was born as the messianic King from David's line. Even in the darkness and waiting, God was faithful to fulfill His promises.

Verse two continues to emphasize the hope that Christ came in the midst of darkness with the repeated phrase "when half-gone was the night." To those who lived between the time of Judah's exile and Christ's birth, it likely seemed as if God had abandoned them. Perhaps the promise of a savior would go unfulfilled. But in the thick darkness of the dead of night, God sent a savior, born of a virgin, just as Isaiah foretold. God showed "His love aright" when it seemed like His love had run out. Jesus Christ came not only during a dark period of Israel's history, but He came in the midst of the darkness of our souls. God indeed had proven His faithfulness to His people.

Jesus Christ is the light of the world who broke through the darkness, and the third verse of this Christmas hymn beautifully illustrates that truth. It may seem as if the darkness and brokenness of this life is too great, but the darkness cannot overcome the glorious light of Christ. The line of this song that says that Christ "dispels with glorious splendor the darkness everywhere" is a reminder that no area of life is beyond the reach of the gospel's light. The gospel changes everything, and when Christ, who is the light, returns, He will make all things new (Revelation 21:5).

We are all people acquainted with darkness. We live in a broken and fallen world, but the light of the world has come and is coming once again to eradicate every bit of darkness. You may feel as if you are in the middle of your own icy winter, or that you are in the deepest darkness of night with no end in sight, but God is faithful even in the dark. Even when it seems as if He is silent, God is working. Even when it seems like He has abandoned you, God is present. God offers incredible hope in the midst of hopelessness. Even when the promises of God are far off, He is working to fulfill every one of them in Christ. That is what we celebrate this Advent season.

EVEN IN THE DARKNESS AND WAITING,

GOD WAS FAITHFUL TO FULFILL HIS PROMISES.

HOW DOES THE IMAGE OF A ROSE BLOOMING IN COLD AND DARKNESS
POINT TO THE HOPE FOUND IN CHRIST?

WHAT SEASON OF DARKNESS HAVE YOU EXPERIENCED OR ARE YOU CURRENTLY EXPERIENCING?
HOW DOES THE WAY THAT CHRIST CAME OFFER HOPE IN YOUR OWN DARKNESS?

READ PSALM 30:5. HOW DOES THIS VERSE GIVE LIGHT TO THE SITUATION
OF THOSE WHO WAITED FOR THE FIRST COMING OF CHRIST?
HOW DOES IT IMPACT YOU AS YOU WAIT FOR HIS SECOND COMING?

THERE'S A SONG IN THE AIR!
THERE'S A STAR IN THE SKY!
THERE'S A MOTHER'S DEEP PRAYER
AND A BABY'S LOW CRY!
AND THE STAR RAINS ITS FIRE
WHILE THE BEAUTIFUL SING, FOR
THE MANGER OF BETHLEHEM
CRADLES A KING!

THERE'S A TUMULT OF JOY
O'ER THE WONDERFUL BIRTH,
FOR THE VIRGIN'S SWEET BOY
IS THE LORD OF THE EARTH.
AY! THE STAR RAINS ITS FIRE
WHILE THE BEAUTIFUL SING,
FOR THE MANGER OF BETHLEHEM
CRADLES A KING!

IN THE LIGHT OF THAT STAR
LIE THE AGES IMPEARLED;
AND THAT SONG FROM AFAR
HAS SWEPT OVER THE WORLD.
EVERY HEARTH IS AFLAME,
AND THE BEAUTIFUL SING
IN THE HOMES OF THE NATIONS
THAT JESUS IS KING!

WE REJOICE IN THE LIGHT,
AND WE ECHO THE SONG
THAT COMES DOWN THROUGH
THE NIGHT FROM THE
HEAVENLY THRONG.
AY! WE SHOUT TO THE LOVELY
EVANGEL THEY BRING, AND
WE GREET IN HIS CRADLE OUR
SAVIOR AND KING!

THERE'S A Song IN THE Air

Advent is a time for believers to look back to the manger in Bethlehem and marvel at the incarnation. In a world infatuated with everything new and improved, it can be difficult to experience wonder over the Christmas story. Though it is a true story of great joy, it is an unchanging story, and familiarity has a way of dulling one's wonder. Yet, year after year, believers around the world marvel at the truth that Jesus came. The virgin conceived and bore a son, just as it was foretold (Isaiah 7:14). Yes, the Redeemer came as a baby, and He was placed in a manger because there was no room in the inn. The Creator of the universe put on flesh and pursued humanity. Though He enjoyed perfect unity and fellowship within the Trinity, He drew near to us while we were still sinners because of His magnificent love!

This hymn carries a playful melody that invites us to marvel at the incarnation. The opening verse reminds people of the magnitude of the truth that the Creator of the universe put on flesh by considering the cosmic juxtaposition between "the star in the sky" and "a baby's low cry." The star bore evidence of God and His provision of the promised Savior. God wielded the universe to make His Son known. His omnipotence was unmistakable alongside His love as evidenced by His willingness to come as a baby. The virgin's baby was the long-awaited King Jesus.

When we understand the incarnation, we cannot help but sing. Worship is the proper response to the good news of Jesus Christ. Consider what happened when the angel appeared before the shepherds and declared the good news. The angel said to them, "Don't be afraid, for look, I proclaim to you good news of great joy that will be for all the people: Today in the city of David a Savior was born for you, who is the Messiah, the Lord. The will be the sign for you: You will find a baby wrapped tightly in cloth and lying in a manger" (Luke 2:10-12). As soon as this glorious message is spoken, the angel is joined by a multitude of heavenly host, and they cannot contain their praise! They break out in song: "Glory to God in the highest heaven, and peace on earth to people he favors!" (Luke 2:14). The angels knew the incarnation is reason to sing!

Consider Mary, the one entrusted to meet the needs of the God-man, and her response to the angel's revelation of God's plan. She went to her cousin Elizabeth's home and sang her song of praise, known as the Magnificat. It begins with "My soul magnifies the Lord, and my spirit rejoices in God my Savior" (Luke 1:46-47). Despite the tangible implications of the supernatural conception that she would face, Mary knew that worship was the proper response to the incarnation. When we, by the Spirit's help, understand the good news of the incarnation, we are compelled to worship.

The Christmas story leads God's people to adoration because it is a stunning story. It is a story that brings hope to our everyday lives. This story is the beautiful song of redemption that has swept over the world. Those with ears to hear this song and respond to it by placing their faith in Jesus Christ experience complete transformation. They are new creations (2 Corinthians 2:17). Their hearts of stone are replaced with hearts of flesh (Ezekiel 11:19, 26:36). Historically, the hearth symbolized the heart of the home. It was the central source of warmth and comfort. When the author wrote "every hearth is aflame and the beautiful sing in the homes of the nations," he was referencing the undeniable renewal of the believer's heart in response to the reconciliation between God and man achieved through Christ, the God-Man. It is a transformation that has a permeating effect.

The incarnation is the stunning truth that God the Son became man in order to reconcile us to God the Father through the power of God the Spirit. This truth that God became man to rescue and redeem His people is a foundational truth that every other aspect of Christian theology depends on. The Christmas story is a story that has stood the test of time. May we respond in worship as we consider how the God who created the universe clothed Himself in humility and came as a baby in pursuit of His people. He identifies with the weak, but He is a strong King who will come again to dwell with His people.

THE INCARNATION IS A REASON TO SING,

NOT JUST ANY SONG, BUT THE SONG OF REDEMPTION.

WHY DOES THE INCARNATION COMPEL BELIEVERS TO WORSHIP?

READ PSALM 34. WRITE THIS PASSAGE INTO A SONG OF PRAISE THAT YOU CAN PRAY.

HOW DOES THE GOSPEL TRANSFORM YOUR HEART?
DO YOU NOTICE A PERMEATING EFFECT OF THIS TRANSFORMATION IN YOUR LIFE?

THE FIRST NOEL THE ANGEL DID SAY
WAS TO CERTAIN POOR SHEPHERDS
IN FIELDS AS THEY LAY; IN FIELDS
WHERE THEY LAY KEEPING THEIR
SHEEP, ON A COLD WINTER'S NIGHT
THAT WAS SO DEEP.

NOEL, NOEL, NOEL, NOEL,
BORN IS THE KING OF ISRAEL.

THEY LOOKED UP AND SAW A STAR
SHINING IN THE EAST, BEYOND THEM
FAR; AND TO THE EARTH IT GAVE
GREAT LIGHT, AND SO IT CONTINUED
BOTH DAY AND NIGHT.

AND BY THE LIGHT OF THAT SAME
STAR THREE WISE MEN CAME FROM
COUNTRY FAR; TO SEEK FOR A KING
WAS THEIR INTENT, AND TO FOLLOW
THE STAR WHEREVER IT WENT.

THIS STAR DREW NIGH TO THE
NORTHWEST, O'ER BETHLEHEM IT
TOOK ITS REST; AND THERE IT DID
BOTH STOP AND STAY, RIGHT OVER
THE PLACE WHERE JESUS LAY.

THEN ENTERED IN THOSE WISE MEN
THREE, FULL REVERENTLY UPON THE
KNEE, AND OFFERED THERE, IN HIS
PRESENCE, THEIR GOLD AND MYRRH
AND FRANKINCENSE.

The First Noel

This familiar hymn at Christmas takes us from the announcement of the baby Jesus being born to a look at the church worshiping, united in one accord by the blood of Jesus.

Noel is a word that finds its root in the French word for Christmas, which comes from the Latin word meaning birthday. The first noel literally means the first Christmas, and this first Christmas was the birthday of Jesus.

On this day, as Luke's Gospel describes, the angels appeared to the shepherds and told them of the birth of a Savior, who was Christ the Lord. The shepherds saw the angels praising God for the birth of Jesus, and once they saw the baby in the manger, they "returned, glorifying and praising God for all the things they had seen and heard."

The song tells of shepherds and wise men who follow the same star, although Scripture does not mention a star in connection with the shepherds. Rather, they hastily made their way to Bethlehem to see the newborn Christ. But the wise men did, in fact, follow a star. Scripture tells us that wise men came from the east, "from country far," to Jerusalem asking, "Where is he who has been born king of the Jews?" They saw the star and came to worship Him. This is significant; they did not ask about the location of a young boy, because they were providentially guided by the star. Their intent was "to seek for a King." Jesus was born as a king! He would not one day become a king, as would have been the case for your average human ruler. This baby was different. He was born a king, with a star heralding His birth beckoning those in distant lands to worship Him.

When Herod heard this, he was "disturbed." Herod was fearful of what this King would bring for him. As Scripture would explain, it was his search for this king that would lead the wise men to the very place where Jesus was born. When the wise men found the boy, they "saw the child with Mary his mother, and falling to their knees, they worshiped him." This is the appropriate response when we come face to face with the King of the Jews, the King of all, who is Jesus. Notice how different this is from Herod's response: Herod feared this Messiah, but the wise men fell to the ground in worship.

The purpose of the wise men coming to see the child was to foreshadow the nations' worship of the Christ. These men were not Israelites. They were probably Persians—practically the end of the earth—coming to hail the King of Israel. Isaiah prophesied about the day this King would arrive:

> *Arise, shine, for your light has come, and the glory of the Lord shines over you. For look, darkness covers the earth, and total darkness the peoples; but the Lord will shine over you, and His glory will appear over you. Nations will come to your light, and kings to the brightness of your radiance.* —Isaiah 60:1-3

When Jesus was born He came to light the whole world, to illumine a world without God by the radiance of His life and work—making plain that the path of salvation would be found in Him. With His birth, glory appeared. This is what makes this first Christmas so joy-filled. And so, with full throats and hearts, we sing, "Noel, Noel, Noel, Noel, Born is the King of Israel!"

THIS BABY WAS DIFFERENT.

HE WAS BORN A KING, WITH A STAR HERALDING

HIS BIRTH BECKONING THOSE IN DISTANT

LANDS TO WORSHIP HIM.

WHY DOES THE BIRTH OF THE KING OF ISRAEL CALL DIFFERENT PEOPLE FROM DIFFERENT PLACES TO RESPOND IN WORSHIP?

READ JOHN 1:3 AND COLOSSIANS 1:15-20. WHY SHOULD WE WORSHIP JESUS?

WRITE A PRAYER OF PRAISE TO GOD FOR SENDING JESUS TO ILLUMINE A WHOLE WORLD WITHOUT GOD.

SILENT NIGHT! HOLY NIGHT!
ALL IS CALM, ALL IS BRIGHT
'ROUND YON VIRGIN MOTHER
AND CHILD. HOLY INFANT,
SO TENDER AND MILD,
SLEEP IN HEAVENLY PEACE,
SLEEP IN HEAVENLY PEACE.

SILENT NIGHT! HOLY NIGHT!
SHEPHERDS QUAKE AT THE SIGHT!
GLORIES STREAM FROM HEAVEN
AFAR, HEAV'NLY HOSTS SING
ALLELUIA;
CHRIST, THE SAVIOR, IS BORN!
CHRIST, THE SAVIOR, IS BORN!

SILENT NIGHT! HOLY NIGHT!
SON OF GOD, LOVE'S PURE LIGHT,
RADIANT BEAMS FROM THY
HOLY FACE, WITH THE DAWN OF
REDEEMING GRACE,
JESUS, LORD, AT THY BIRTH,
JESUS, LORD, AT THY BIRTH.

SILENT NIGHT! HOLY NIGHT!
WONDROUS STAR, LEND THY LIGHT;
WITH THE ANGELS LET US SING
ALLELUIAS TO OUR KING;
CHRIST, THE SAVIOR, IS BORN!
CHRIST, THE SAVIOR, IS BORN!

Silent Night

———

A central truth of the gospel and a cornerstone of the Christian faith is the deity of Christ. In fact, the Christmas story hinges on that doctrine. Jesus Christ was fully God and fully man. He had a real divine nature and a real human nature. God the Son put on flesh in order to reconcile us to God the Father through the power of God the Spirit. That is the wondrous essence of the incarnation, and it is encapsulated beautifully in the phrase "holy infant" in this classic Christmas hymn. It is a phrase that can only be attributed to Jesus Christ. Due to the reality of original sin, there is no other infant that can claim that title.

In His incarnation, Jesus "emptied himself" (Philippians 2:7). This does not mean He renounced His deity. Instead, He willingly emptied Himself of certain divine privileges. And as He renounced certain divine attributes, He took on all essential human attributes, including basic human needs and weaknesses. This was made evident that holy night when He entered the world as a baby. He relied on His mother, Mary, for nutrition and care. He was exposed to all of the natural elements of this world. Imagine that evening: the noise and odor of farm animals, the feel of the swaddle against the straw in the manger, and the warmth conducted from the embrace of His earthly parents. He was the Light of the world that pierced through the darkness on that ordinary night. Jesus knew the end of the story because He was fully God, but what about Mary?

Mary was a new mom. She fully experienced the physical and emotional effects of giving birth. She was also outside of the comforts of her own home! How was she processing this monumental event in the history of mankind? Scripture does not tell us too many details of the experience from her perspective, but we get a small glimpse in Luke 2. Scripture tells us that after the shepherds were visited by the angel and told the good news of the birth of Christ, they hastily went to Bethlehem (Luke 2:16). They were amongst the first visitors of the new family of three. Immediately, they "reported the message they were told about this child" (Luke 2:17). In the following verses, we are told the responses of those who heard. First, everyone who heard were amazed (verse 18). Awe and wonder are appropriate responses to the incarnation. Then, we are told Mary's response in verse 19, which reads,

"Mary was treasuring up all these things in her heart and meditating on them." The weight of the incarnation did not escape her.

Mary knew it was a holy night. Though she was young, it was evident that she was a thinking woman. Mary responded to the incarnation in a way we all should: with wonder and awe fueled by a deep understanding of the magnitude of the incarnation. More likely than not, it was the opposite of a silent night that sacred evening. The air was probably filled with Mary's groans as she endured labor pangs mixed with a cacophony of farm animals excited by their unexpected visitors. It was then filled with visitors and newborn cries. Yet, in the midst of it all, Mary took note of the details. She hid them in her heart and pondered them. She remembered what the angel Gabriel told her, "He will be great and will be called the Son of the Most High" and "He will reign over the house of Jacob forever, and his kingdom will have no end." (Luke 1:32-33). She knew the child to be born would be called holy because He was the Son of God. She knew He was a holy infant indeed.

This Christmas, in the midst of all the holiday festivities and cheer, may we respond to the glorious birth of Christ with wonder and awe that is fueled by a deep understanding of the magnitude of the incarnation. May we remember how the heavenly hosts responded to the incarnation and join singing, "Alleluia! Christ the Savior is born!" We may not have many silent nights, but may we quiet our hearts this Advent season and remember that the eternal Son of God took on human flesh to offer redeeming grace to His people.

He is Jesus, Lord at His birth.

HE WAS THE LIGHT OF THE WORLD THAT PIERCED THROUGH THE DARKNESS ON THAT ORDINARY NIGHT.

WHY IS IT IMPORTANT THAT JESUS WAS A HOLY INFANT?

READ LUKE 1:46-55. HOW DID MARY RESPOND TO THE INCARNATION?

WHAT CAN YOU DO THIS HOLIDAY SEASON TO QUIET YOUR HEART TO REMEMBER THE BEAUTY OF THE INCARNATION? HOW WOULD THAT AFFECT YOUR WORSHIP?

O LITTLE TOWN OF BETHLEHEM,
HOW STILL WE SEE THEE LIE; ABOVE
THY DEEP AND DREAMLESS SLEEP
THE SILENT STARS GO BY:
YET IN THY DARK STREETS SHINETH
THE EVERLASTING LIGHT; THE HOPES
AND FEARS OF ALL THE YEARS
ARE MET IN THEE TONIGHT.

FOR CHRIST IS BORN OF MARY,
AND GATHERED ALL ABOVE, WHILE
MORTALS SLEEP, THE ANGELS KEEP
THEIR WATCH OF WOND'RING LOVE.
O MORNING STARS, TOGETHER
PROCLAIM THE HOLY BIRTH! AND
PRAISES SING TO GOD THE KING,
AND PEACE TO MEN ON EARTH.

HOW SILENTLY, HOW SILENTLY,
THE WONDROUS GIFT IS GIV'N!
SO GOD IMPARTS TO HUMAN HEARTS
THE BLESSINGS OF HIS HEAV'N.
NO EAR MAY HEAR HIS COMING,
BUT IN THIS WORLD OF SIN, WHERE
MEEK SOULS WILL RECEIVE HIM
STILL, THE DEAR CHRIST ENTERS IN.

O HOLY CHILD OF BETHLEHEM,
DESCEND TO US, WE PRAY;
CAST OUT OUR SIN AND ENTER IN;
BE BORN IN US TODAY. WE HEAR
THE CHRISTMAS ANGELS
THE GREAT GLAD TIDINGS TELL;
O COME TO US, ABIDE WITH US,
OUR LORD EMMANUEL!

O Little TOWN OF Bethlehem

Before time began, God had a plan of redemption. It was a plan that included the use of the weak and foolish things of this world. It was a plan that included a costly pursuit of mankind—a cost that only God could afford. It was a plan that was initiated by God the Father as an overflow of the perfect unity, fellowship, and love experienced within the Trinity. It was a plan that God the Son accomplished through His life, death, and resurrection. And it is a plan that is sustained and applied even now by God the Spirit.

As we spend time this Advent season looking back to His first coming, may we be struck afresh by the peculiar glory woven into this plan. The God who created the universe put on flesh and came as a baby. And this baby was born in a manger, not a palace or even a home. This baby was born to a young virgin and a humble carpenter, not well-established, prominent members of society. This baby was born in the little town of Bethlehem, not Jerusalem. Yet, this baby was the fulfillment of prophecy (Isaiah 7:14, Micah 5:2). This baby—Jesus—was the long-awaited Messiah. He was the promised Redeemer.

The birth of Jesus reminds us that our God is in the details, and the details attest to the truth that God is the divine author of this grand story of redemption. Only He could foresee the twists and turns and still dot the "i's" and cross the "t's." He is sovereign, and this incommunicable attribute is put on display even by His providential selection of where Jesus would be born. This hymn is a familiar melody to many of us. But what really is the significance of Bethlehem? And more importantly, what does it teach us about God?

Bethlehem was indeed a small town about six miles south of Jerusalem. It was the geographic location of many stories that are the threads that create the grand tapestry of the story of Scripture. Rachel, Jacob's wife, was buried in Bethlehem, which was formerly called Ephrath (Genesis 35:19). It was the primary setting of the book of Ruth (Ruth 1:19). It was the birthplace of David (1 Samuel 17:12), and the place where he would later be anointed king (1 Samuel 16:1). Most notably, Bethlehem was the clan of Judah that the prophet Micah foretold would be the birthplace of the Messiah (Micah 5:2). And it was!

As the first stanza in this hymn notes, "In the dark street shineth the Everlasting Light; the hopes and fears of all the years are met in Thee tonight." It was hundreds of years of waiting, but God orchestrated events in a way only He could, and the Messiah entered the world just as He said He would. He used ordinary means—a political census—to bring Mary and Joseph (descendants of David) to Bethlehem. It was a grueling trek over seventy miles through mountainous terrain from Nazareth to Bethlehem. But time, distance, and human ability were factors, not constraints, to the fulfillment of the promises of God. Thus, Bethlehem reminds us that God keeps His promises. Our fears can be replaced with faith in a God who proves Himself faithful.

Furthermore, in His infinite wisdom, God chose to write a story layered with beauty. We can trust Him and be co-heirs with Him! But this story He wrote also shows us how He works. He chooses what is foolish in the world to shame the wise; He chooses what is weak in the world to shame the strong; He chooses the things the world deems insignificant and places significance on them. He does this "so that no one may boast in his presence" (1 Corinthians 1:29). God's aim is to magnify His own glory, even by His choosing of a little town and by His choosing of us.

Bethlehem, the manger, and Mary and Joseph—they all testify to this truth. We testify to this truth as well. We are merely jars of clay, ordinary and expendable. Yet, we have this treasure—the gospel—to show "that this extraordinary power may be from God and not from us" (2 Corinthians 4:7). As this hymn notes, we are "meek souls" in whom "the dear Christ enters in." He is the Giver and the "wondrous Gift" given to us. He imparts to human hearts—to jars of clay—the blessings of His heaven. We are entrusted the gospel; we have the indwelling Holy Spirit!

So as we press in and feel the weight of the waiting and longing for the coming of the promised Messiah in the town of Bethlehem, may we be strengthened in our current season of waiting and longing for His return. Just as Bethlehem, the least of the clans of Judah, was divinely chosen for the glory of God, we are as well. He is Immanuel—He has come to us, and He will come again to dwell with His people forever.

JESUS WAS THE LONG-AWAITED MESSIAH.

HE WAS THE PROMISED REDEEMER.

WHAT DO WE LEARN ABOUT GOD WHEN WE CONSIDER HIS PROVIDENTIAL SELECTION OF BETHLEHEM IN THE CHRISTMAS STORY?

HOW DOES THE WAY THAT GOD WORKS ENCOURAGE YOU TO TRUST HIM?

READ 2 CORINTHIANS 4:7-11. HOW DOES THE TRUTH THAT GOD IS THE POTTER AND YOU ARE A JAR OF CLAY IMPACT HOW YOU LIVE?

Week Two Reflection

PARAPHRASE THE PASSAGES FROM THIS WEEK.

_____

_____

_____

_____

_____

_____

**WHAT DID YOU OBSERVE FROM THIS WEEK'S TEXT
ABOUT GOD AND HIS CHARACTER?**

_____

_____

_____

_____

_____

_____

WHAT DO THESE PASSAGES TEACH ABOUT THE CONDITION
OF MANKIND AND ABOUT YOURSELF?

_____

_____

_____

_____

_____

_____

HOW DO THESE PASSAGES POINT TO THE GOSPEL?

_____

_____

_____

_____

_____

_____

HOW SHOULD YOU RESPOND TO THESE PASSAGES?
WHAT IS THE PERSONAL APPLICATION?

_____

_____

_____

_____

_____

_____

WHAT SPECIFIC ACTION STEPS CAN YOU TAKE THIS WEEK TO
APPLY THESE PASSAGES?

_____

_____

_____

_____

_____

_____

WEEK THREE
DAY ONE

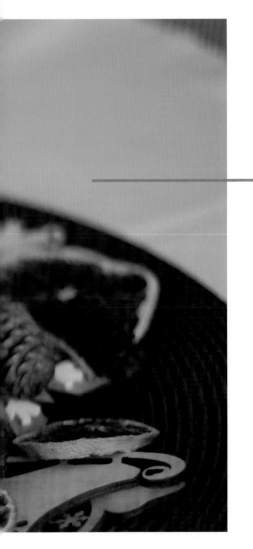

CANDLE LIGHTING DAY

The Joy Candle

According to tradition, a candle will be lit this week to symbolize joy. This is a wonderful reminder to us in the Advent season of where our joy is found. Joy is not found in anything other than Jesus Himself. This week's memory verse reminds us that our joy is not hinged on our circumstances, but that it is fully dependent on Jesus. Because Jesus is our joy, we can have joy in every situation. We can rejoice as we wait and hope expectantly for God's faithfulness. We have joy because of who He is. Jesus is our joy.

ROMANS 12:12

Rejoice in hope;
be patient
in affliction;
be persistent
in prayer.

IN THE BLEAK MIDWINTER,
FROSTY WIND MADE MOAN,
EARTH STOOD HARD AS IRON,
WATER LIKE A STONE;
SNOW HAD FALLEN, SNOW ON
SNOW, SNOW ON SNOW, IN THE
BLEAK MIDWINTER, LONG AGO.

OUR GOD, HEAVEN CANNOT
HOLD HIM, NOR EARTH SUSTAIN;
HEAVEN AND EARTH SHALL FLEE
AWAY WHEN HE COMES TO REIGN.
IN THE BLEAK MIDWINTER A
STABLE PLACE SUFFICED, THE LORD
GOD ALMIGHTY, JESUS CHRIST.

ANGELS AND ARCHANGELS MAY
HAVE GATHERED THERE,
CHERUBIM AND SERAPHIM
THRONGED THE AIR;
BUT HIS MOTHER ONLY, IN
HER MAIDEN BLISS,
WORSHIPED THE BELOVED
WITH A KISS.

WHAT CAN I GIVE HIM,
POOR AS I AM? IF I WERE A
SHEPHERD, I WOULD BRING A LAMB;
IF I WERE A WISE MAN, I WOULD
DO MY PART; YET WHAT I CAN I
GIVE HIM: GIVE MY HEART.

IN THE *Bleak* *Midwinter*

Most of our winter days could be descried as a bleak midwinter, couldn't it? Maybe it has been a very long day, or month, or year. Maybe it has been a very long season clouded by the dreariness of this world, which relentlessly pounds upon your soul.

There is irony in the hymn writer's use of snow to convey dreariness, given that snow is often used to invoke memories of happier days. We remember the youthful excitement of seeing snow in the morning as a kid, hoping that school was cancelled for the day. We long for feelings of elation captured by snowball fights, sledding and hot chocolate. Yet during the bleak midwinter, we see it as only "snow on snow, snow on snow," a cold, windy and howling winter. As C.S. Lewis so fittingly wrote, it can feel like it's "always winter, never Christmas."

So what hope do we have on days when darkness clings to our souls? We remember Christ, who endured this bleak midwinter on our behalf, destroying its power and bringing us the hope of spring. During His life, Jesus endured betrayal, hunger, thirst, and conflict. He was abandoned by those closest to Him. Though worthy of worship from all creation, He clothed Himself in humility and endured the deepest of sorrows. Christ could have come in a mighty display of power, beaming down from the sky. He could have come with stars bursting, demanding the awe and worship of all who saw Him. Instead, He humbled Himself and was born in a lowly manger to a poor Jewish girl. He who receives praise from angels is worthy of our worship, but when He came to earth, not even the inn-keepers took notice. Christ knew that He would not receive the worship that He deserved, and yet lived a life full of contentment, joy, and obedience, perfectly submitted to the Father's will.

When the angels appeared to the shepherds that night, it had been a bleak midwinter for the Jews. God had not spoken to His people for hundreds of years. There was silence, longing, and darkness. In the midst of a world filled with grief, fear, anger, and despair, the angels came that precious night pronouncing good news of great joy (Luke 2:10). God broke through the silence, bringing an announcement that would change the world, pronouncing that One was coming who would make all things right. Christ's light broke through the darkness as He made a way for us to be right with God, and offered abundant life to all who trust in Him.

No longer do we need to live in fear, wondering if God is pleased with us. No longer do we need to constantly strive or hide in shame. The God who sees all things also provided a way for us to be saved from our guilt. He is the wisest of all. He knew the fears and doubts of His closest friends. He knew the anger and disgust of the Pharisees, though masked in spirituality. He knew that He would die. Those whom He came to save not only doubted Him and questioned Him, but they also abandoned Him. And yet, Christ made a way. To all who believe, no matter how bad their past or how much they have sinned, Christ offers complete healing and forgiveness. Christ bore our sins on the cross, paying the penalty of death that we deserved (Romans 6:23), and offering freedom to all who trust in Him.

When we are clouded by lingering feelings of shame, we need look only to Christ and remember that He bore it for us, and gave us His perfect record. In dark seasons, we remember that He is enough for angels, and He is more than enough for our longing hearts. We cry out with the Psalmist, "Who do I have in heaven but you? And I desire nothing on earth but you. My flesh and my heart may fail, but God is the strength of my heart, my portion forever" (Psalm 73:25-26). He is our comfort in times of sorrow, and our light in the darkness.

How can we respond to such a beautiful Redeemer? We gladly "give Him our hearts" as the song proclaims, and offer our lives as living sacrifices to Him (Romans 12:1). Now that our greatest debt has been paid, we are called to live in righteousness, fully satisfied in the goodness of Christ. We are called to a new affection, a new contentment in Christ alone. He bore our sins on His body so that we might die to sin, and live for righteousness (1 Peter 2:24). He has become our Good Shepherd, gently guiding us. He endured the darkest winter on our behalf. In our seasons of winter, we can rejoice and remember that Christ came in such a season as this.

HE HAS THAWED OUR HEARTS, FROZEN IN

THE BLEAK MIDWINTER. HE IS WORTHY,

BEAUTIFUL, HOLY. HE IS GOD COME NEAR. HE IS KING.

HOW DID CHRIST FULFILL THE BLEAK MIDWINTER ON OUR BEHALF?

READ I PETER 2:21-25. HOW DOES THIS ENCOURAGE YOU IN SUFFERING?

ARE THERE ANY AREAS WHERE YOU STRUGGLE TO ACCEPT THE LORD'S FORGIVENESS?
WRITE OUT A PRAYER OF CONFESSION TODAY, AND THANK THE LORD FOR
BEARING OUR GUILT AND SHAME.

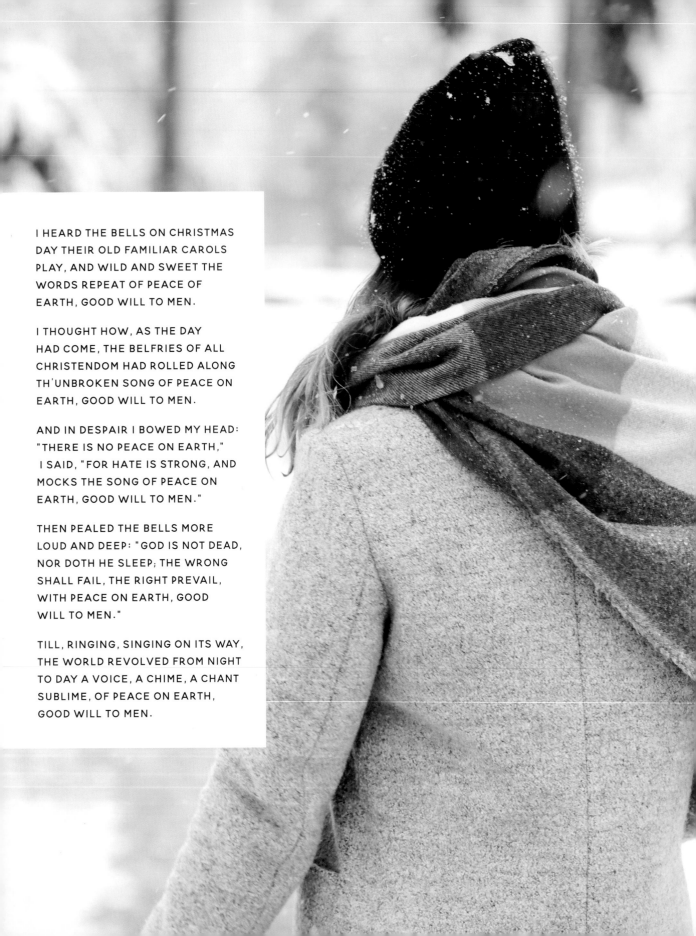

I HEARD THE BELLS ON CHRISTMAS DAY THEIR OLD FAMILIAR CAROLS PLAY, AND WILD AND SWEET THE WORDS REPEAT OF PEACE OF EARTH, GOOD WILL TO MEN.

I THOUGHT HOW, AS THE DAY HAD COME, THE BELFRIES OF ALL CHRISTENDOM HAD ROLLED ALONG TH'UNBROKEN SONG OF PEACE ON EARTH, GOOD WILL TO MEN.

AND IN DESPAIR I BOWED MY HEAD: "THERE IS NO PEACE ON EARTH," I SAID, "FOR HATE IS STRONG, AND MOCKS THE SONG OF PEACE ON EARTH, GOOD WILL TO MEN."

THEN PEALED THE BELLS MORE LOUD AND DEEP: "GOD IS NOT DEAD, NOR DOTH HE SLEEP; THE WRONG SHALL FAIL, THE RIGHT PREVAIL, WITH PEACE ON EARTH, GOOD WILL TO MEN."

TILL, RINGING, SINGING ON ITS WAY, THE WORLD REVOLVED FROM NIGHT TO DAY A VOICE, A CHIME, A CHANT SUBLIME, OF PEACE ON EARTH, GOOD WILL TO MEN.

Read: Psalm 121, Psalm 34:18, Isaiah 53:5, Luke 2:14, Colossians 1:19-20

I Heard The Bells

ON CHRISTMAS DAY

———

Singing is part of the celebration of the Christmas season. We sing at our church services. We sing in our homes. We hear songs overhead as we scurry through our Christmas shopping and hum along. With all of the carols, hymns, and songs we hear at Christmas time, we might be left to wonder what the stories are behind the songs that we sing?

A particularly surprising story lies behind this Christmas carol. On Christmas day in 1863, a man by the name of Henry Wadsworth Longfellow wrote a poem that resonated deeply with his own heart and personal observances around him. Nearly two years prior, Henry's wife died tragically after her dress caught on fire. He had awoken from his sleep to find her inflamed and tried to extinguish the best he could, even with his own body, but the burns were too severe. She died the morning of July 10, 1861, and Henry Longfellow's bodily burns were so critical that he was unable even to attend his wife's funeral. He was left widowed with six children.

Surrounding that time Henry's son, Charles Appleton Longfellow, ran away to Washington D.C. to join President Lincoln's Union army to fight in the Civil War. This war would become the bloodiest war in American history. In 1863, news arrived to Henry that his son had been seriously wounded. He was shot through the left shoulder and the bullet had skimmed his spine. Nearly paralyzed, surgeons gave hopeful news of recovery to come.

Longfellow writes of the ringing bells on that following December day, and the songs of proclamation singing, "peace on earth, goodwill to men!" Clearly, a difficult sentiment to share in when all around him spoke of loss, tragedy, and injustice. The lyrics seemed to mock his situation with optimism. But as the words continue, the theme of listening despite feeling brings about hope amid despair.

The heart of the lyrics he wrote for "I Heard the Bells on Christmas Day" was heavy and burdensome, yet the final stanza ends triumphantly:

Then pealed the bells more loud and deep:
God is not dead, nor doth he sleep;
The wrong shall fail, the right prevail,
with peace on earth, good-will to men.

These words speak of the hope found in the midst of our hardest moments. God is not absent from them. God is near and present. A psalmist reminds us that, "He will not allow your foot to slip; your Protector will not slumber. Indeed, the Protector of Israel does not slumber or sleep" (Psalm 121:3-4). Oftentimes when we face opposition and we look around the world, and we see the evil winning, sin is prospering, we may be tempted to think that God is not acting as we think He should. But we must trust that He is not dead. He does not sleep. Nothing happens apart from not only His knowledge, but His willing it to be. Therefore, we can trust that when all is said and done, the wrong shall fail and the right shall prevail.

So when unspeakable trials come in this life, we can rest in the truth that Christ has come to bring us peace. Isaiah prophesies, "But he was pierced because of our rebellion, crushed because of our iniquities; punishment for our peace was on him, and we are healed by his wounds" (Isaiah 53:5). Jesus Christ purchased peace for us with His life, so that we could be assured at every moment, through every circumstance, that there is hope beyond what we see now. That hope is the promise for all to be right in the world when Jesus returns, fully and finally restoring peace on earth.

WE CAN TRUST THAT WHEN ALL IS SAID AND DONE, THE WRONG SHALL FAIL AND THE RIGHT SHALL PREVAIL.

PEACE ON EARTH COMES AT A COST. READ ISAIAH 53:5 AND COLOSSIANS 1:22-23.
HOW DID JESUS CHRIST PURCHASE PEACE FOR US NOW AND FOREVER?

THOUGH THE WORLD AROUND US MAY FEEL CHAOTIC, BROKEN, AND ANYTHING BUT PEACEFUL,
WHAT COMFORT DO WE HAVE WHILE WE WAIT FOR CHRIST TO COME AGAIN? READ PSALM 121.

HOW CAN THIS HYMN ENCOURAGE US DURING TRIAL AND TRAGEDY TO
FIND REST AND HOPE IN OUR SAVIOR?

IN THE LITTLE VILLAGE OF
BETHLEHEM, THERE LAY A CHILD
ONE DAY, AND THE SKY WAS
BRIGHT WITH A HOLY LIGHT O'ER
THE PLACE WHERE JESUS LAY.

ALLELUIA! O HOW THE ANGELS
SANG. ALLELUIA! HOW IT RANG!
AND THE SKY WAS BRIGHT WITH
A HOLY LIGHT, 'TWAS THE
BIRTHDAY OF A KING.

'TWAS A HUMBLE BIRTH-PLACE,
BUT O HOW MUCH GOD GAVE TO
US THAT DAY, FROM THE MANGER
BED WHAT A PATH HAS LED,
WHAT A PERFECT, HOLY WAY.

ALLELUIA! O HOW THE ANGELS
SANG. ALLELUIA! HOW IT RANG!
AND THE SKY WAS BRIGHT WITH
A HOLY LIGHT, 'TWAS THE
BIRTHDAY OF A KING.

Birthday of A King

Often our appreciation of something can be amplified when contrasted with other opposing things. Think of the bright stars scattered across the night sky, colorful flowers popping out of the dusky dirt or radiant colors painted on a blank canvas. In this hymn written by William H. Neidlinger in 1890, we are reminded of how God establishes beauty by placing two opposing ideas together when He presents the Savior of the world, Jesus Christ, as a king born in the most unlikely way.

The words found in this hymn bring to a focus the small and simple elements of the glorious day when Jesus Christ was born. Consider the town of Bethlehem. In Micah 5, the prophet foretold that the Messiah would come from the small and seemingly insignificant town:

> *Bethlehem Ephrathah, you are small among the clans of Judah; one will come from you to be ruler over Israel for me. His origin is from antiquity, from ancient times. Therefore, Israel will be abandoned until the time when she who is in labor has given birth; then the rest of the ruler's brothers will return to the people of Israel. He will stand and shepherd them in the strength of the Lord, in the majestic name of the Lord his God. They will live securely, for then his greatness will extend to the ends of the earth. —Micah 5:2–4*

In the Old Testament, Bethlehem served as an early Canaanite settlement connected with the patriarchs. The noteworthy story of Ruth, Naomi, and Boaz took place primarily in the town of Bethlehem. King David, the great-grandson of Ruth and Boaz grew up in Bethlehem and the town eventually became known as the City of David as a mark of his great dynasty. At the time of Jesus' birth, Bethlehem had declined into a small, meager village. Three gospel accounts record this town as the place of Jesus' birth. Caesar Augustus issued a decree that a census would be taken of everyone in the Roman world at that time. So Joseph, coming from the line of David, went to Bethlehem to be registered with Mary. While there, by God's sovereign ordinance, Jesus was born.

Jesus' birth took place in a stable and He was laid as a newborn in a manger. Likely due to the overcrowding caused by the census, the inn was too full and therefore the unrefined stable was the only place available to the couple. Mary and Joseph would take shelter with the animals before she gave birth.

You might think God's only Son deserved a more regal and high-profile place of birth. You might assume His entrance should have been more extravagant and elegant. Many who were waiting for this birth expected these very things. Instead, the Savior of the world was born into a quiet and common stable. And yet, this birth speaks of a glorious God, enthroned in the heavens, who would make a way to come to us. The meekness of His birth makes Him available to us so that we might draw near to approach Him. Jesus' entrance was not announced in a prominent city or even first shared to the great and royal. This message of the Savior born was first told by angels to the lowliest and least regarded of that day, shepherds, keeping watch over their flock by night. It was that night the promise of a Messiah had been fulfilled. Immanuel had come to them.

His humble birth would lead to a humble life. Jesus Christ came to save us. He walked in obedience even to the point of death on a cross. In all of His glory and majesty, Jesus became a servant so that we could become children of God. He came to make a way for us to be reunited with the Father. He took on flesh so that we might be clothed with His righteousness. He bore the wrath we deserve so we could be lavished with His grace. The birth of King Jesus reveals the heart of God. He has given the greatest gift of all to the least deserving of all.

Though a humble birth that holy night, He would leave this world in victory. He defeated death, rose from the grave, and was exalted to the right hand of God who has "highly exalted him and gave him the name that is above every name, so that at the name of Jesus every knee will bow—in heaven and on earth and under the earth—and every tongue will confess that Jesus Christ is Lord, to the glory of God the Father" (Philippians 2:9-11). Now we celebrate His birth every Christmas season with glory and honor and praise, perfectly fitting for the birthday of our King.

THE MEEKNESS OF HIS BIRTH MAKES HIM AVAILABLE TO US SO THAT WE MIGHT DRAW NEAR TO APPROACH HIM.

HOW DOES THIS HYMN DRAW ATTENTION TO THE HUMILITY OF JESUS CHRIST
THE KING REPRESENTED THROUGH HIS BIRTH?

CHRIST CAME IN AN UNEXPECTED WAY. MANY ASSUMED HE WOULD HAVE A MAJESTIC
BIRTH AND BECOME A STRONG RULER OF THE DAY. BUT GOD WAS PURPOSEFUL IN HOW
HE WOULD PRESENT THE SAVIOR TO THE WORLD. HOW DOES I CORINTHIANS 1:26-29
SPEAK INTO JESUS' HUMBLE ENTRANCE?

HOW CAN WE FIND COMFORT TO DRAW NEAR IN UNDERSTANDING JESUS CHRIST
AS OUR HUMBLE KING?

AWAY IN A MANGER, NO CRIB FOR
A BED, THE LITTLE LORD JESUS
LAID DOWN HIS SWEET HEAD;
THE STARS IN THE NIGHT SKY
LOOKED DOWN WHERE HE LAY,
THE LITTLE LORD JESUS ASLEEP
ON THE HAY.

THE CATTLE ARE LOWING, THE
BABY AWAKES, BUT LITTLE LORD
JESUS, NO CRYING HE MAKES.
I LOVE THEE, LORD JESUS,
LOOK DOWN FROM THE SKY
AND STAY BY MY CRADLE 'TIL
MORNING IS NIGH.

BE NEAR ME, LORD JESUS;
I ASK THEE TO STAY CLOSE BY ME
FOREVER AND LOVE ME, I PRAY.
BLESS ALL THE DEAR CHILDREN
IN THY TENDER CARE, AND FIT
US FOR HEAVEN, TO LIVE WITH
THEE THERE.

Away IN A Manger

The overarching message woven throughout the Old Testament is this: He is coming. The New Testament is the consummation of that message because He has come. Jesus has come, and this is good news of great joy for all people (Luke 2:10). But by the start of the New Testament, it had been over 400 years since the last prophecy in the Old Testament. Most people believed God was silent during those years. Maybe they even felt forgotten. But Scripture shows us that though the voice of God was withdrawn during those years, the hand of God never stopped working. He was in charge of the course of events that took place during those centuries. In fact, there was not a single event beyond His control. And at the ordained time, the Light of the world pierced through the darkness in the form of a baby. He was born in the town of Bethlehem, just as it was foretold (Micah 5:2). He was from the line of David (Isaiah 9:6-7) and from the tribe of Judah (Genesis 49:10). Every detail was a part of His plan—even the manger.

The manger has become a focal point during the Christmas season. It is the centerpiece of nativities, holding baby Jesus. We also sing about the manger in this familiar carol that sings like a lullaby. Perhaps the portrayal of Jesus as a baby in the first two stanzas invites us to identify with the God-man. It is true that He became like us so that He might save us. He put on flesh to accomplish the will of His Father and close the chasm between our unrighteousness and His holiness. He is our High Priest who is able to sympathize with our weaknesses (Hebrews 4:15).

As we consider the manger this season, may our hearts and minds dwell on the beauty of the incarnation. The manger reminds us of the deity of Christ. He was fully God and fully man. This is essential because it was the means by which He accomplished the will of God. While remaining fully God, He put on human nature. He "laid down His sweet head" on the manger. He was "asleep on the hay." He was awakened by the lowing of the cattle. And though the song says otherwise, because He was fully man, He cried like any other baby.

But He did not put on our sin nature. Instead, He lived a life of perfection in order to atone for the sins of His people. So as we consider the wooden manger, may we remember the wooden cross. As He humbly entered into the world as a baby, He also humbled Himself by dying on the cross. In turn, may we clothe ourselves in humility and take up our crosses. May we not seek the comforts of this world, but remember that at His birth, Jesus did not have a crib to lay His head. Instead, He had an uncomfortable manger full of hay. He later echoes this in adulthood when He says, "the Son of Man has no place to lay his head" (Matthew 8:20, Luke 9:58). May we remember this is not our home. Like Christ, we are sojourners in this land.

The good news is this: we are not alone. In our season of waiting, we have the indwelling Holy Spirit. We have the Word of God and the people of God. We have access to the throne of grace to receive grace and mercy through prayer. We can sing the prayer that makes up the last stanza with those truths in mind: "Be near me, Lord Jesus; I ask Thee to stay close by me forever and love me, I pray. Bless all the dear children in Thy tender care, and fit us for heaven, to live with Thee there."

When we remember the wooden manger this season, may we remember that He came to dwell with us. What costly love that was displayed from the manger to the cross! We look to His righteousness that makes us "fit" for heaven to live with Him for all of eternity. And in our current waiting, we look to our union with Christ to empower us to trust, obey, and love. We partner with the Spirit as He sanctifies us and transforms us to be made more into Christlikeness, from one degree of glory to another (2 Corinthians 3:18). And we turn our gaze to behold Him, looking forward to the day when we will see His glory perfectly.

EVERY DETAIL WAS A PART OF HIS PLAN,

EVEN THE MANGER.

HOW DOES THE MANGER LEAD YOU TO REMEMBER THE CROSS?

HOW DOES THE PERSON AND WORK OF JESUS CHRIST IMPACT HOW YOU LIVE?

WHEN YOU ARE SEEKING THE COMFORTS OF THIS WORLD,
HOW CAN THE MANGER REMIND YOU TO TURN YOUR GAZE TO ETERNITY?

WHAT CHILD IS THIS, WHO, LAID TO
REST, ON MARY'S LAP IS SLEEPING?
WHOM ANGELS GREET WITH
ANTHEMS SWEET, WHILE
SHEPHERDS WATCH ARE KEEPING?

THIS, THIS IS CHRIST, THE KING,
WHOM SHEPHERDS GUARD AND
ANGELS SING: HASTE, HASTE TO
BRING HIM LAUD, THE BABE, THE
SON OF MARY!

WHY LIES HE IN SUCH MEAN
ESTATE, WHERE OX AND ASS
ARE FEEDING? GOOD CHRISTIAN,
FEAR: FOR SINNERS HERE THE
SILENT WORD IS PLEADING.

SO BRING HIM INCENSE, GOLD,
AND MYRRH, COME, PEASANT,
KING TO OWN HIM. THE KING OF
KINGS SALVATION BRINGS; LET
LOVING HEARTS ENTHRONE HIM.

What Child is This?

The beautiful melody of this familiar carol ushers us to the moment in time where Mary sat in a stable after giving birth to her son. We can imagine the baby in Mary's lap. It kindles an awe within us that this baby would be born in a stable, but this was not just any baby—it was Jesus, the very Son of God. To respond to the question, "What Child is this?" is to declare that the very Son of God has come as flesh, being born as a baby. And that is something that causes us to stop in reverence of the incarnation.

The wonder of the incarnation is that God—who hollowed out the ocean's depths and crafted mountain heights—would be born as a needy, helpless child surrounded by dirty animals like an ox and an ass. The hymn describes this as a "mean estate," pressing into service a use of "mean" that is archaic for us, but which carries the sense of humble, shabby, inferior. As one pastor has put it, "When the Son of God came down from heaven, he came all the way down." Truly the Son of God did not consider equality with God something to be held onto, and for our sakes, He emptied Himself and took the form of a servant.

The Word was made flesh in order that He could dwell among us, to live life like we do, with both the joys and the pains. Jesus assumed all of our humanity so that He might redeem all of humanity. Even as an infant this was Jesus' mission, and silently the Word-made-flesh was pleading, urging that sinners would be reconciled to God.

To redeem and reconcile us, he suffered and paid for our sins. You see, His lowly entrance into the world foreshadowed the depth that He would humble Himself to—the ridicule, the beatings, the cross, and finally, His death. Nails and spear would pierce him through as he bore the cross, for me and for you. He took on flesh to die for us, standing in our place and dying as our substitute. We are the sinners. We are the ones who deserve death because of our sins, but Jesus, though perfectly sinless, took on our sin and died our death so that we might gain His righteousness. What makes Jesus' birth beautiful and wondrous is its glorious condescension, a humility seen most clearly in the cross.

With such a sacrifice, He deserves the worship of both kings and peasants. He is the Savior of all who will believe, irrespective of class and any number of the other distinctives that normally separate humanity—race, gender, nationality. He is the King of Kings whose right-ruling place is the throne of every human heart. And because of His great mercy, human hearts should be eager to lovingly enthrone Him.

The shepherds' response was exactly right—they ran with haste to bring Him laud. What else could the revelation of such a stunningly humble King evoke, besides eager and delighted praise? All of creation had been waiting for this moment, and so the announcement of the babe's birth was accompanied by angels' songs and joyously awe-filled declarations. Christmas is the season we similarly behold the child and wonder. We wonder that God would become like us. We wonder that He would stoop so low. We wonder that He would die in our place on the cross. And we move from wonder to wide-eyed worship, joining along with a virgin's lullaby and angels' anthems our own joyous praise at the birth of the babe, the son of Mary.

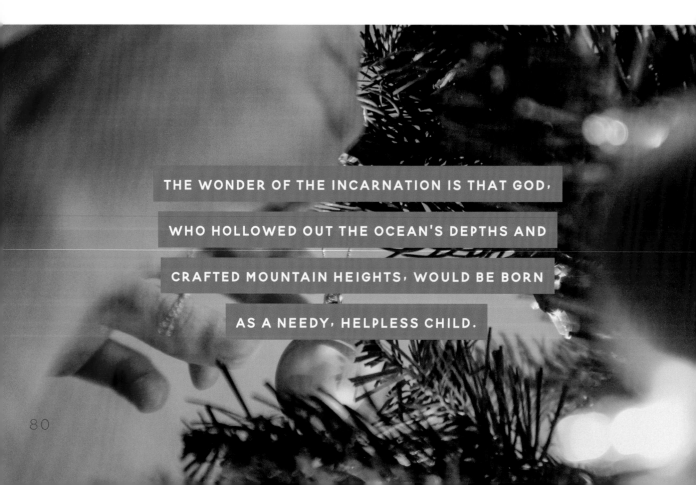

THE WONDER OF THE INCARNATION IS THAT GOD, WHO HOLLOWED OUT THE OCEAN'S DEPTHS AND CRAFTED MOUNTAIN HEIGHTS, WOULD BE BORN AS A NEEDY, HELPLESS CHILD.

WHAT DID IT LOOK LIKE FOR JESUS TO EMPTY HIMSELF AND TAKE ON FLESH?

WHAT PAIN AND STRUGGLES HAVE YOU HELD ON TO THAT YOU THINK IS
TOO GREAT FOR THE LORD? READ HEBREWS 4:15. HOW DOES THIS ENCOURAGE YOU
TO TRUST THE LORD WITH THESE STRUGGLES?

WRITE A PRAYER OF JOY THAT CHRIST IS BORN.

Week Three Reflection

PARAPHRASE THE PASSAGES FROM THIS WEEK.

_____
_____
_____
_____
_____
_____

WHAT DID YOU OBSERVE FROM THIS WEEK'S TEXT
ABOUT GOD AND HIS CHARACTER?

_____
_____
_____
_____
_____

WHAT DO THESE PASSAGES TEACH ABOUT THE CONDITION
OF MANKIND AND ABOUT YOURSELF?

_____
_____
_____
_____
_____

HOW DO THESE PASSAGES POINT TO THE GOSPEL?

_____

_____

_____

_____

_____

HOW SHOULD YOU RESPOND TO THESE PASSAGES?
WHAT IS THE PERSONAL APPLICATION?

_____

_____

_____

_____

_____

WHAT SPECIFIC ACTION STEPS CAN YOU TAKE THIS WEEK TO
APPLY THESE PASSAGES?

_____

_____

_____

_____

_____

WEEK FOUR
DAY ONE

CANDLE LIGHTING DAY

The Love Candle

For the fourth week of Advent, a candle is lit to symbolize love. This Advent season, may we be left overwhelmed by the matchless and initiating love of God that is made visible to us through the incarnation. 1 John 4:9 declares for us that God's love has been made manifest among us through God sending His Son to die so that we might live. The advent season is a reminder of waiting and a reminder of hope that was yearning for the fulfillment of the Messiah. It is also a reminder that in His sovereign love God fulfills our every longing and hope through Jesus our Savior.

I JOHN 4:9

*God's love was
revealed among us
in this way: God sent
his one and only Son
into the world so that we
might live through him.*

HARK! THE HERALD ANGELS SING,
"GLORY TO THE NEWBORN KING:
PEACE ON EARTH, AND MERCY MILD,
GOD AND SINNERS RECONCILED!"
JOYFUL, ALL YE NATIONS, RISE,
JOIN THE TRIUMPH OF THE SKIES;
WITH ANGELIC HOSTS PROCLAIM,
"CHRIST IS BORN IN BETHLEHEM!"

HARK! THE HERALD ANGELS SING,
"GLORY TO THE NEWBORN KING"

CHRIST, BY HIGHEST HEAVEN
ADORED, CHRIST, THE EVERLASTING
LORD, LATE IN TIME BEHOLD HIM
COME, OFFSPRING OF THE VIRGIN'S
WOMB: VEILED IN FLESH THE
GODHEAD SEE; HAIL TH'INCARNATE
DEITY, PLEASED WITH US IN FLESH
TO DWELL, JESUS, OUR IMMANUEL.

HAIL THE HEAVEN-BORN PRINCE
OF PEACE! HAIL THE SUN OF
RIGHTEOUSNESS! LIGHT AND LIFE
TO ALL HE BRINGS, RISEN WITH
HEALING IN HIS WINGS. MILD HE
LAYS HIS GLORY BY, BORN THAT
MAN NO MORE MAY DIE, BORN TO
RAISE US THE SONS OF EARTH,
BORN TO GIVE US SECOND BIRTH.

Read: Isaiah 9:6, Matthew 1:22-25, Hebrews 1:1-2

Hark! The HERALD Angels Sing

Christmas does not come easy for everyone. Many find the holidays to be a harsh reality of their suffering and hardships as the world around them carries on with the celebration. This is why we must hold fast to the biblical reason for the season. Singing our theology is an important concept in Christian worship. When we are singing to God and about God, we must be assured that the things we sing about are true. So as we sing the hymns and songs of Christmas, may we listen closely and cling tightly to the comfort found in the words that point us towards the true reason for the season.

Charles Wesley's hymn, "Hark! The Herald Angels Sing" brings light to an important theological concept—the incarnation of Jesus Christ. The incarnation refers to the eternal Son of God putting on flesh. The doctrine of incarnation teaches that the Son of God took on humanity in the person of Jesus Christ, being fully divine (Colossians 2:9) and fully human (John 1:6). The beautiful hymn accentuates this theological truth:

Christ, by highest heaven adored,
Christ, the everlasting Lord,
late in time behold him come,
offspring of the Virgin's womb:

Veiled in flesh the Godhead see;
hail the incarnate Deity,
pleased with us in flesh to dwell,
Jesus, our Immanuel.

In the beginning, the Son of God reigns with the Father and the Spirit. He is enthroned in the heavens. Everything that was made was made by Him, through Him, and to Him. He lives in a loving, perfect, and harmonious communal relationship within the Trinity.

He is not made of a material substance, not confined by time and space, and not limited. But from the beginning of time, God's providential and sovereign plan was to send His Son to the world. When the curse of sin came through the actions of Adam and Eve in the garden of Eden, the salvation of humanity would come at a price. Priests and kings, though some valiant and faithful, could never save us from the destruction we had caused. We proved time and time again that we could not save ourselves. Even in our best efforts, we were disobedient and led astray. There is no one without sin to purify us from our unrighteousness, no not one.

We need a true Savior, a righteous Savior who is not just merely a man. We need a Savior who can serve as a mediator between us and God. We need a Savior who can bridge the divide between our sin and God's holiness. So God, in His deep love and kindness, sent Jesus Christ, fully God and fully man, to intercede for us (2 Timothy 2:5). He became a fetal ball in the dark womb of the virgin Mary, now confined to space and time. Though He spoke the world into existence, He became an infant, limited in speech and mobility. Though He possessed all power and authority and dominion, He grew to be a child, following rules, listening to authority, and learning and growing through the years.

There is only One who can pay the price for our sins—One who was veiled in flesh and perfectly righteous in all of His ways. It is the only way for humanity to be reconciled back to God (Acts 4:12). Jesus Christ took on that penalty and brought us salvation through His life, death, and resurrection. Through it all, He remained faithful to the will of His Father. Not only did He do this in obedience to the Father, but Jesus Christ was pleased with us in flesh to dwell. He delights in saving us!

What does an understanding of the incarnation mean to us? It means God the Son entered earth in flesh and dwelt among us. He is not far away or distant. He does not leave us to ourselves. He came to us. He draws near to us. He lived and walked among us. He was tempted as we are tempted. He suffered as we suffer. He is a High Priest who can sympathize with our weaknesses (Hebrews 4:15). It is because of these truths that we can sing, "Jesus, Our Immanuel!" because God is actually with us (Matt. 1:23).

Even when life is hard, our circumstances are not ideal, and we have faced unspeakable trials, we can sing the message shared by the angels every Advent season. We can proclaim with unwavering confidence in the hope that was revealed that holy night in Bethlehem—Jesus is our eternal living God! Because God came to us, we know that He will never leave us or forsake us. Because the prophecies of Christ were fulfilled, we know that He will always keep His promises. Because He sought a relationship with us through the ultimate sacrifice, we know that His love for us is unending. We can face every doubt, fear, temptation, and sorrow, knowing that our tomorrow is filled with hope and our forever rests secure in the one and only Savior, Jesus Christ.

WHY DO THE FULL HUMANITY AND FULL DIVINITY OF JESUS MATTER FOR OUR SALVATION?

WHAT DOES AN UNDERSTANDING OF THE INCARNATION TEACH US ABOUT GOD?
HOW DOES IT LEAD US TO WORSHIP HIM?

HOW CAN WE HAVE HOPE AMIDST TRIAL AND SUFFERING?

ANGELS WE HAVE HEARD ON HIGH,
SWEETLY SINGING O'ER THE PLAINS,
AND THE MOUNTAINS IN REPLY
ECHO BACK THEIR JOYOUS STRAINS.

GLORIA IN EXCELSIS DEO,
GLORIA IN EXCELSIS DEO.

SHEPHERDS, WHY THIS JUBILEE?
WHY YOUR JOYOUS STRAINS
PROLONG? WHAT THE GLADSOME
TIDINGS BE, WHICH INSPIRE YOUR
HEAV'NLY SONG?

GLORIA IN EXCELSIS DEO,
GLORIA IN EXCELSIS DEO.

COME TO BETHLEHEM AND SEE
HIM WHOSE BIRTH THE ANGELS
SING; COME, ADORE ON BENDED
KNEE CHRIST THE LORD, THE
NEWBORN KING.

Angels We HAVE HEARD On High

It was nighttime. Many of us may have a hard time imagining a night sky without the lights from a city, but here, the shepherds were in the field in complete darkness. The only light that shone in the dark night's sky was that of the stars. This night was not unlike any night that the shepherds had in the days before. They were carrying out the responsibilities of being shepherds as they tended to their sheep both day and night. So with sheep scattered around them, the shepherds would have settled in for the night.

But in a very routine moment, the skies broke forth and a great light shone around them. An angel stood before these men and the glory of the Lord shone around them. This is the very glory of God Himself. This bright light is the very light that surrounds the presence of God and in this moment, the shepherds are able to see the glory of the Lord with their very own eyes in the middle of a field while they are taking care of sheep.

They were terrified. And you could imagine why they would be. The normalcy of this night was interrupted to make an announcement, and that announcement would change the world. But they did not know what would come from this interaction with an angel. Their faces reflected the terror and fear that filled their hearts. And to this, the angel spoke, "Fear not."

The angel did not come to ignite fear in their hearts but to proclaim good news of great joy that will be for all the people. This good news was not news of an ordinary birth. This was the birth of the Savior. This was Jesus Christ the Lord. And with that the angels proclaimed, "Glory to God in the highest!" If the multitude of angels could not contain their joy, then how much more joy must the shepherds have had who heard and then saw the birth of the

Savior? We learn in the following verse that after seeing Christ, "The shepherds returned, glorifying and praising God for all the things they had seen and heard, which were just as they had been told" (Luke 2:20).

We can sense the joy that the shepherds had, and it was not rooted in the fact that they had seen an angel face to face, but it was that they went and saw the Christ. Everything they saw and heard was just as it had been told to them. The Christ was born and they could not contain their joy.

And here we are, reading of these shepherds thousands of years later—this instant recorded for us to read over and over. But let us not lose the magnitude of the moment recorded for us. God chose to reveal His glorious plan—the birth of His Son, Jesus Christ the Lord—to these ordinary men. And this same truth has been revealed to us. Jesus, the Christ, is born! He has come and our appropriate response is to adore Him on bended knee. For He is, indeed, the newborn King.

This is why we sing, "Glory to God in the highest." We are singing because Christ the Lord, the Savior of the world, has come. We can imagine the multitude of angels singing, "Glory to God in the highest heaven, and peace on earth to people he favors." And as we gather together in our homes and churches throughout the season, may we marvel in the words "Gloria, in excelsis Deo," as we echo the songs of the multitude of angels praising God and giving Him glory. For He has come.

HE HAS COME AND OUR APPROPRIATE RESPONSE IS TO ADORE HIM ON BENDED KNEE. FOR HE IS, INDEED, THE NEWBORN KING.

WHY DO YOU THINK GOD CHOSE TO REVEAL THE BIRTH OF HIS SON TO SHEPHERDS IN A FIELD?

WHAT WOULD HAVE BEEN OUR NATURAL RESPONSE TO A MULTITUDE OF ANGELS?

WHAT GIVES US JOY? ULTIMATE JOY CAN ONLY COME FROM KNOWING CHRIST.
HOW HAVE YOU MISPLACED JOY IN YOUR OWN LIFE?

JOY TO THE WORLD! THE LORD
IS COME: LET EARTH RECEIVE
HER KING; LET EV'RY HEART
PREPARE HIM ROOM,
AND HEAV'N AND NATURE SING,
AND HEAV'N AND NATURE SING,
AND HEAV'N, AND HEAV'N AND
NATURE SING.

JOY TO THE EARTH! THE SAVIOR
REIGNS: LET MEN THEIR SONGS
EMPLOY; WHILE FIELDS AND
FLOODS, ROCKS, HILLS, AND PLAINS
REPEAT THE SOUNDING JOY,
REPEAT THE SOUNDING JOY,
REPEAT, REPEAT THE SOUNDING JOY.

NO MORE LET SINS AND SORROWS
GROW, NOR THORNS INFEST THE
GROUND; HE COMES TO MAKE
HIS BLESSINGS FLOW
FAR AS THE CURSE IS FOUND,
FAR AS THE CURSE IS FOUND,
FAR AS, FAR AS THE CURSE IS FOUND.

HE RULES THE WORLD WITH
TRUTH AND GRACE, AND MAKES
THE NATIONS PROVE THE GLORIES
OF HIS RIGHTEOUSNESS
AND WONDERS OF HIS LOVE,
AND WONDERS OF HIS LOVE,
AND WONDERS, WONDERS OF
HIS LOVE.

Joy to THE World

"Joy to the World" is perhaps one of the most well known and most beloved Christmas songs, and it celebrates the joy that the advent of Jesus Christ brings. Tucked into the original version of this Isaac Watts hymn are these lines telling the beautiful gospel message:

> *No more let sin and sorrow grow*
> *Nor thorns infest the ground:*
> *He comes to make his blessings flow*
> *Far as the curse is found.*

The words embody the ultimate hope of the gospel, that while the reaches of the curse of sin were devastatingly expansive, Christ will bring complete renewal and restoration.

The reason that Christ's coming is something to celebrate is because He makes His blessings known as far as the curse is found, but just how far is that? The curse given as a result of Adam and Eve's sin in Genesis 3 brought physical and emotional pain. It meant conflict and broken relationships. The curse infected the physical world and brought strife and hardship in labor. The curse was a curse of death, and not only physical death, but also spiritual death. Sin has devastating consequences, and the curse of sin infects every corner of creation. We see it in every bit of brokenness, every disease, and every injustice. It is evident in the grief we experience in response to the loss of a loved one or in a strained relationship. All of the pain and suffering in this world finds its root in sin, and the curse of sin leaves no area of life untouched.

The joy of this song is the fulfillment of a promise that goes all the way back to Genesis 3:15, when God promised that He would send a redeemer to crush the head of the serpent. This promise was the sure hope that Jesus Christ would come to reverse the curse. Christ's first coming brings the firstfruits of renewal, pointing to the day when He will eradicate sin and its curse. During Jesus' earthly ministry, the partial restoration that He brought prefigured the complete transformation to come. His miraculous healings point to the day when sickness will be obliterated. The casting out of demons is a foretaste of a world completely purged of evil. The physical resurrections envision the resurrection of the dead when Christ returns.

The birth of Jesus Christ that we celebrate at Christmastime brought incredible blessings. He freed us from the power of sin and gave us new life in Him, but His first coming was just the beginning. The hope of the gospel is not just in this life, but in the next. Revelation 21 shows a vision of a future reality, a day when the resurrected Christ who is seated at the right hand of the Father returns again to bring what He started to its consummation. It is on that day that we will receive our King at last, and the blessings that Christ brings will truly flow far as the curse is found as Jesus declares, "Look, I am making everything new" (Revelation 21:5). The pain and death and mourning of the fall will be forgotten as God draws near to wipe away every tear from our eyes. The thorns of the curse will infest the ground no longer, and joy will abound.

For some of us, singing the words of this familiar carol may seem stale. We look around this world and we are acutely aware that the curse is still very much at work. How can we honestly sing of joy for all the world when our lives are plagued with suffering? Perhaps the hope of the gospel does not seem so hopeful when we look at the reality of our own lives. If the joyful sentiment of this hymn falls flat in our hearts, it may be that we have an incomplete hope. The scope of the gospel is not limited to what we can see now, but the end of the story is that everything will be gloriously transformed. We can rejoice not because everything is as it should be, but because we have the assurance that it will not always be this way. The hope of Christmas is not just hope for today, but the hope of eternity. When our hearts grab hold of that hope, we can truly sing "Joy to the world!" because we know where the story is headed.

THE HOPE OF CHRISTMAS IS NOT JUST

HOPE FOR TODAY, BUT THE HOPE OF ETERNITY.

HOW DO YOU SEE EVIDENCE OF THE CURSE OF GENESIS 3 IN YOUR LIFE AND IN THE WORLD?

COMPARE GENESIS 3 TO REVELATION 21:1-5. HOW DOES CHRIST'S SECOND COMING
ADDRESS THE CURSE?

IN THIS SEASON WHERE WE SING ABOUT JOY, IS JOY SOMETHING THAT SEEMS ACCESSIBLE
OR DIFFICULT TO COME BY? HOW CAN HAVING AN ETERNAL MINDSET IMPACT YOUR JOY?

O COME, ALL YE FAITHFUL,
JOYFUL AND TRIUMPHANT, O COME
YE, O COME YE TO BETHLEHEM;
COME AND BEHOLD HIM BORN
THE KING OF ANGELS;

O COME LET US ADORE HIM,
O COME LET US ADORE HIM,
O COME LET US ADORE HIM,
CHRIST THE LORD.

SING, CHOIRS OF ANGELS,
SING IN EXULTATION, O SING,
ALL YE BRIGHT HOSTS OF HEAV'N
ABOVE; GLORY TO GOD,
ALL GLORY IN THE HIGHEST;

YEA, LORD, WE GREET THEE,
BORN THIS HAPPY MORNING,
JESUS, TO THEE BE ALL GLORY
GIV'N; WORD OF THE FATHER,
NOW IN FLESH APPEARING;

O COME LET US ADORE HIM,
O COME LET US ADORE HIM,
O COME LET US ADORE HIM,
CHRIST THE LORD.

O Come
ALL YE
Faithful

During this Advent season, we have beheld the glory of Christ in the Word of God. We have read about the One who fulfills every promise of God. We have seen beautiful mysteries of God's eternal plan of redemption revealed in the incarnation of Jesus Christ. Now this song beckons us to join in the song of all creation as we worship the One who was born the King of angels. When we see the beauty of the gospel set before us, our response should be adoration and worship for the One who was born to pay the price of our redemption. We were created to worship God and to ascribe to Him the glory that He is due, and true worship of the Lord produces authentic joy in our hearts (Isaiah 43:21, Psalm 29:2).

The words of "O Come All Ye Faithful" are reminiscent of the exhortation of Psalm 95, in which David calls us to worship and bow down before the Lord. The words of this psalm point us to Christ who is worthy of all our worship. We sing to Him because He has accomplished our salvation. He makes a way for man to dwell in God's presence, and He is the King over all who is ruling and will reign forever. He has existed eternally as the Son of God and through Him all things were made (John 1:3). He is the Good Shepherd who laid down His life for us (John 10:11). And so, we sing praises to Him, we worship Him, we kneel before Him and bow down because He is the Lord our God who gave Himself for us.

Expressing adoration and praise to God in response to what He has done should not just be something that we do with our words, but worship should be the ongoing reality of our entire lives. The word rendered worship in the Old Testament is the Hebrew word *shachah*, which has the meaning of bowing down or prostration before the Lord. Likewise, the Greek word *proskyneō* that is translated as worship in the New Testament denotes a prostration, kneeling down, or kissing of a hand. Worship, then, is not simply declaring God's praise, although it certainly includes proclaiming His goodness, but serving and honoring God in love and humility. Paul explains in Romans 12 that our spiritual worship is done through offering ourselves up to the Lord as a living sacrifice, walking in obedience to His commands. So, as we embark into a new year, we worship Christ as we extend His love and forgiveness to those around us. We glorify Him as we turn from our sin and pursue holiness by His power. We proclaim our adoration to Him as we walk in His ways by His grace.

Jesus said in John 4:24 that true worshipers worship in Spirit and in truth. True worship for God overflows from a heart that has been filled with the Spirit and transformed by the truth of the gospel, and so we must draw near to the One who is the Truth and who gives us His Spirit. We cannot worship what we do not love, and we cannot love what we do not know, so we seek to know Him as we pursue Him in His Word, not just during Advent, but every day.

Christ has come! He has purchased our redemption and washed away our sins with His blood. He has humbled Himself and drawn near to us as one of us. He was born to die for us that we might live, and new life is ours in Christ Jesus. Let all the faithful come and adore the glorious King! Let us come together in joy knowing that He has won the victory! Christ has triumphed over sin and death, and we can rejoice in the good news that He who has overcome the world has united Himself to us. O come let us adore Him!

WORSHIP SHOULD BE THE ONGOING REALITY OF OUR ENTIRE LIVES.

HOW HAS BEHOLDING CHRIST THIS ADVENT SEASON STIRRED YOUR HEART TO WORSHIP?

HOW DOES OUR RESPONSE OF WORSHIP GO BEYOND SINGING SONGS OR DECLARING
THE GOODNESS OF GOD? WHAT ARE SOME TANGIBLE WAYS YOU COULD WORSHIP
THROUGH YOUR ACTIONS IN YOUR OWN LIFE?

WORSHIP IS CULTIVATED AS WE GROW IN OUR KNOWLEDGE AND LOVE FOR GOD.
HOW CAN YOU SEEK TO KNOW HIM MORE THIS WEEK?

GO, TELL IT ON THE MOUNTAIN
OVER THE HILLS AND EVERYWHERE
GO, TELL IT ON THE MOUNTAIN
THAT JESUS CHRIST IS BORN

WHILE SHEPHERDS KEPT THEIR
WATCHING O'ER SILENT FLOCKS
BY NIGHT, BEHOLD THROUGHOUT
THE HEAVENS THERE SHONE A
HOLY LIGHT

GO, TELL IT ON THE MOUNTAIN
OVER THE HILLS AND EVERYWHERE
GO, TELL IT ON THE MOUNTAIN
THAT JESUS CHRIST IS BORN

THE SHEPHERDS FEARED AND
TREMBLED WHEN LO! ABOVE THE
EARTH RANG OUT THE ANGELS
CHORUS THAT HAILED THE
SAVIOR'S BIRTH

GO, TELL IT ON THE MOUNTAIN
OVER THE HILLS AND EVERYWHERE
GO, TELL IT ON THE MOUNTAIN
THAT JESUS CHRIST IS BORN

DOWN IN A LOWLY MANGER
THE HUMBLE CHRIST WAS BORN
AND GOD SENT US SALVATION
THAT BLESSED CHRISTMAS MORN

Go Tell
IT ON THE
Mountain

John Wesley Work II was the son of an African American church choir director and scholar in Nashville, Tennessee. He grew up watching his father sing in church choirs and introducing spiritual music to members of the Fisk Jubilee Singers. John II acquired a love for music and history, himself, becoming a composer, singer, collector of spiritual folk music, and eventually a professor of history and Latin.

There is still a question as to where exactly the song "Go Tell It On the Mountain" originated, but John II and the Work family were the first to bring it to life and recognition. This song is a powerful piece that marvels at the glorious message of Jesus' birth given to the lowly shepherds of the day. In the 1880s the Fisk Jubilee Singers would perform the anthem-like piece as one of their hit songs. The preservation of this song has brought its infectious melody to us today.

The message of this song holds the real power and highlights the reverberating effect of the good news shared that night. The announcement of the birth of Jesus Christ compelled its hearers to speak of this good news. From the moment of Christ's birth, the angels announce the glorious news to the shepherds in the fields. "Today in the city of David a Savior was born for you, who is the Messiah, the Lord. This will be the sign for you: You will find a baby wrapped tightly in cloth and lying in a manger" (Luke 2:11-12). The shepherds then continued to tell of this good news to all who would hear them. The Bible does not say the shepherds were concerned about what others would think about the news or how they would respond. It does not say the shepherds waited for the right moment to share what they had heard. They simply shared the truth of what they had seen and heard. "After seeing them, they reported the message they were told about this child, and all who heard it were amazed at what the shepherds said to them" (Luke 2:17-18).

Not only were the shepherds encouraged to spread the message, but so are God's people. Jesus Christ invited us into the kingdom-building work of the Great Commission, commanding us to, "Go, therefore, and make disciples of all nations, baptizing them in the name of the Father and of the Son and of the Holy Spirit, teaching them to observe everything I have commanded you. And remember, I am with you always, to the end of the age" (Matthew 28:19-20).

As those who have become witnesses to the saving work of Jesus Christ, we are called to carry the truth of salvation to all who will hear it. The good news of the gospel is that God sent His only Son to save us from the wrath that we deserved by His death on the cross and united us with the Father in righteousness both now and forevermore. If you are a Christian, you understand that this is the very message that brought you salvation. This is the very message that brought you from death to life. This is the very message that has given you imperishable hope in Jesus. The profound implications of this truth should not be kept to ourselves but should compel us to respond as the shepherds responded—to share the truth of what we have seen and heard without hesitation.

The Advent season is filled with recollections and teachings of Christ's birth and its implications. Even throughout this study, we have visited and explored hymns and songs that shine a light on that glorious truth. But as we read and hear of this good news time and time again, may it never fall dull on our ears. May it never leave our affections unstirred. This Advent season, may the good news of Jesus Christ coming to the world to save sinners like you and me, absolutely astound and amaze us. May it light our eyes with childlike wonder. May it warm our hearts to know the depth of the Father's love for us to send His only Son. And may it kindle in us an eager desire to carry this good news to anyone and everyone who will listen, so that they could be changed by it, too. May the message we hear compel us to go and tell it on the mountain, over the hills and everywhere that our Savior, Jesus Christ was born.

AS THOSE WHO HAVE BECOME WITNESSES TO THE SAVING WORK OF JESUS CHRIST, WE ARE CALLED TO CARRY THE TRUTH OF SALVATION TO ALL WHO WILL HEAR IT.

HOW ARE YOUR AFFECTIONS MOST STIRRED BY THE GOSPEL? HOW CAN YOU TAKE INTENTIONAL
TIME THIS ADVENT SEASON TO ENJOY AND CELEBRATE THE GOOD NEWS?

IN WHAT WAYS ARE YOU ENCOURAGED AND CHALLENGED BY THE SHEPHERDS TO SHARE
THE GOOD NEWS OF THE GOSPEL TO THOSE WHO HAVE NOT HEARD?

WRITE A PRAYER ASKING GOD TO EMPOWER AND EMBOLDEN YOU WITH SHARING THE GOOD NEWS
OF THE GOSPEL THIS SEASON AND ALL YEAR LONG. NAME SPECIFIC PEOPLE IN YOUR PRAYER
AND ASK GOD TO PROVIDE AN OPPORTUNITY!

Week Four Reflection

PARAPHRASE THE PASSAGES FROM THIS WEEK.

_____

_____

_____

_____

_____

_____

**WHAT DID YOU OBSERVE FROM THIS WEEK'S TEXT
ABOUT GOD AND HIS CHARACTER?**

_____

_____

_____

_____

_____

_____

WHAT DO THESE PASSAGES TEACH ABOUT THE CONDITION
OF MANKIND AND ABOUT YOURSELF?

_____

_____

_____

_____

_____

_____

HOW DO THESE PASSAGES POINT TO THE GOSPEL?

_____

_____

_____

_____

_____

_____

HOW SHOULD YOU RESPOND TO THESE PASSAGES?
WHAT IS THE PERSONAL APPLICATION?

_____

_____

_____

_____

_____

_____

WHAT SPECIFIC ACTION STEPS CAN YOU TAKE THIS WEEK TO
APPLY THESE PASSAGES?

_____

_____

_____

_____

_____

_____

HYMNS *of the* SEASON

What Child is This?

What Child is this, who, laid to rest, On Ma-ry's lap is sleep-ing?

Whom an-gels greet with an-thems sweet, While shep-herds watch are keep-ing?

This, this is Christ, the King, Whom shep-herds guard and an-gels sing:

Haste, haste to bring Him laud, The Babe, the Son of Ma-ry!

Come Thou Long Expected Jesus

Come, Thou long ex-pect-ed Je-sus, Born to set Thy people free; From our fears and sins re-lease us; Let us find our rest in Thee. Is-rael's strength and con-so-la-tion, Hope of all the earth Thou art; Dear de-sire of ev-'ry na-tion, Joy of ev-'ry long-ing heart.

Go Tell It on the Mountain

Go, tell it on the moun-tain, O-ver the hills and ev-'ry-where;

Go, tell it on the moun-tain That Je-sus Christ is born!

While shep-herds kept their watch-ing O'er si-lent flocks by night,

Be-hold through-out the heav-ens There shone a ho-ly light.

Hark the Herald Angels Sing

I Heard the Bells on Christmas Day

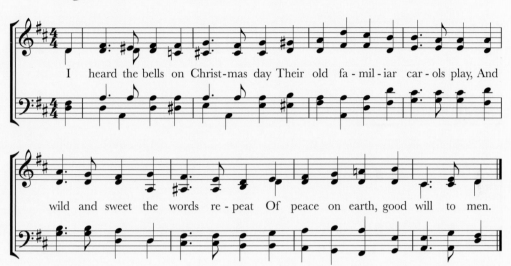

I heard the bells on Christ-mas day Their old fa - mil - iar car - ols play, And

wild and sweet the words re - peat Of peace on earth, good will to men.

Joy to the World

Joy to the world! the Lord is come; Let earth re - ceive her King; Let ev - 'ry heart pre - pare Him room, And heav'n and na - ture sing, And heav'n and na - ture sing, And heav'n,__ and heav'n and na - ture sing.

And heav'n and na - ture sing, And heav'n and na - ture sing,

O Come, O Come Emmanuel

O come, O come, Em - man - u - el, And ran - som cap - tive Is - ra - el, That mourns in lone - ly ex - ile here, Un - til the Son of God ap - pear. Re - joice! Re - joice! Em - man - u - el Shall come to thee, O Is - ra - el!

Silent Night

The First Noel

The first No - el the an - gel did say, Was to cer - tain poor
shep - herds in fields as they lay; In fields where they lay keep - ing their
sheep, On a cold win - ter's night that was so deep. No - el, No -
- el, No - el, No - el, Born is the King of Is - ra - el.

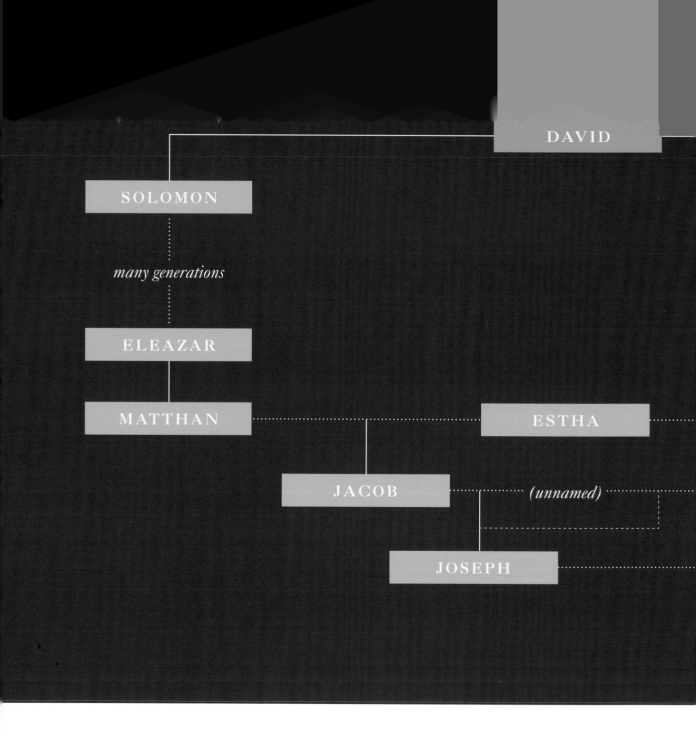

DAVID

SOLOMON

many generations

ELEAZAR

MATTHAN

ESTHA

JACOB

(unnamed)

JOSEPH

JEREMIAH 23:5-6

"LOOK, THE DAYS ARE COMING" — THIS IS THE LORD'S DECLARATION — "WHEN I WILL RAISE UP A RIGHTEOUS BRANCH FOR DAVID. HE WILL REIGN WISELY AS KING AND ADMINISTER JUSTICE AND RIGHTEOUSNESS IN THE LAND. IN HIS DAYS JUDAH WILL BE SAVED, AND ISRAEL WILL DWELL SECURELY. THIS IS THE NAME HE WILL BE CALLED: THE LORD IS OUR RIGHTEOUSNESS."

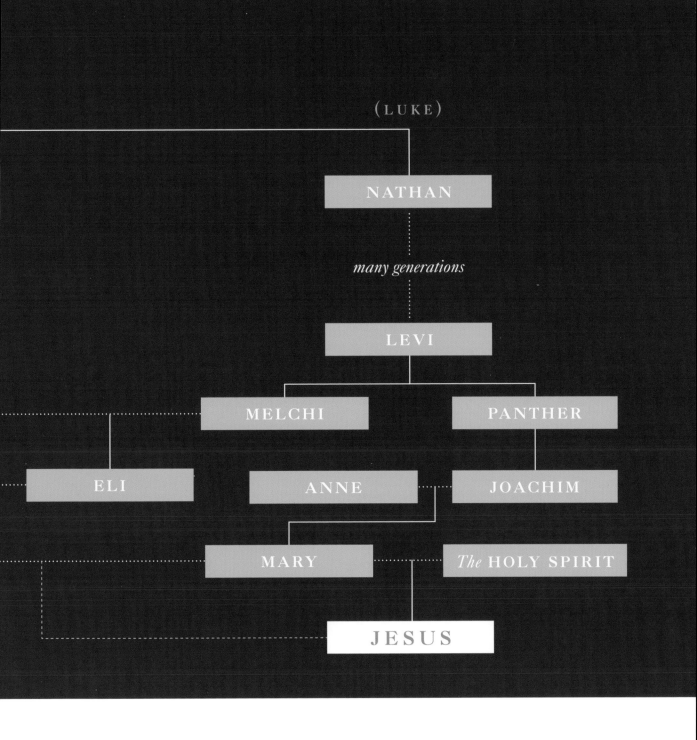

(LUKE)

NATHAN

many generations

LEVI

MELCHI

PANTHER

ELI

ANNE

JOACHIM

MARY

The HOLY SPIRIT

JESUS

LUKE 1:32-33

HE WILL BE GREAT AND WILL BE CALLED THE SON OF THE MOST HIGH, AND THE
LORD GOD WILL GIVE HIM THE THRONE OF HIS FATHER DAVID. HE WILL REIGN
OVER THE HOUSE OF JACOB FOREVER, AND HIS KINGDOM WILL HAVE NO END.

Music in the Bible

CEREMONIES & CELEBRATIONS

The Dedication of the Temple
2 Chronicles 5:13a

The trumpeters and singers joined together to praise and thank the LORD with one voice. They raised their voices, accompanied by trumpets, cymbals, and musical instruments, in praise to the LORD: For he is good; his faithful love endures forever...

The Dedication of the Jerusalem Walls
Nehemiah 12:27

At the dedication of the wall of Jerusalem, they sent for the Levites wherever they lived and brought them to Jerusalem to celebrate the joyous dedication with thanksgiving and singing accompanied by cymbals, harps, and lyres.

FOR THE GOOD OF GOD'S PEOPLE

Ephesians 5:19

speaking to one another in psalms, hymns, and spiritual songs, singing and making music with your heart to the Lord

Colossians 3:16

Let the word of Christ dwell richly among you, in all wisdom teaching and admonishing one another through psalms, hymns, and spiritual songs, singing to God with gratitude in your hearts.

PRAISING GOD FOR WHO HE IS AND WHAT HE'S DONE

Psalm 95:2

Let us enter his presence with thanksgiving; let us shout triumphantly to him in song.

Psalm 105:2

Sing to him, sing praise to him; tell about all his wondrous works!"

Psalm 98:4-7

Let the whole earth shout to the LORD; be jubilant, shout for joy, and sing. Sing to the LORD with the lyre, with the lyre and melodious song. With trumpets and the blast of the ram's horn shout triumphantly in the presence of the LORD, our King. Let the sea and all that fills it, the world and those who live in it, resound.

Psalm 150:3-6

Praise him with the blast of a ram's horn; praise him with harp and lyre. Praise him with tambourine and dance; praise him with strings and flute. Praise him with resounding cymbals; praise him with clashing cymbals. Let everything that breathes praise the LORD. Hallelujah!

THE EARLY CHURCH

Acts 16:25

About midnight Paul and Silas were praying and singing hymns to God, and the prisoners were listening to them.

MUSIC IN ETERNITY

Revelation 14:3

They sang a new song before the throne and before the four living creatures and the elders, but no one could learn the song except the 144,000 who had been redeemed from the earth.

What is
the Gospel

Thank you for reading and enjoying this study with us!

We are abundantly grateful for the Word of God, the instruction we glean from it, and the ever-growing understanding about God's character from it. We're also thankful that Scripture continually points to one thing in innumerable ways: the gospel.

WHAT IS THE GOSPEL?

We remember our brokenness when we read about the fall of Adam and Eve in the garden of Eden (Genesis 3), when sin entered into a perfect world and maimed it. We remember the necessity that something innocent must die to pay for our sin when we read about the atoning sacrifices in the Old Testament. We read that we have all sinned and fallen short of the glory of God (Romans 3:23), and that the penalty for our brokenness, the wages of our sin, is death (Romans 6:23). We all are in need of grace and mercy, but most importantly, we all need a Savior.

We consider the goodness of God when we realize that He did not plan to leave us in this dire state. We see His promise to buy us back from the clutches of sin and death in Genesis 3:15. And we see that promise accomplished with Jesus Christ on the cross. Jesus Christ knew no sin yet became sin so that we might become righteous through His sacrifice (2 Corinthians 5:21). Jesus was tempted in every way that we are and lived sinlessly. He was reviled, yet still yielded Himself for our sake, that we may have life abundant in Him. Jesus lived the perfect life that we could not live, and died the death that we deserved.

The gospel is profound yet simple. There are many mysteries in it that we can never exhaust this side of heaven, but there is still overwhelming weight to its implications in this life. The gospel is the telling of our sinfulness and God's goodness, and this gracious gift compels a response. We are saved by grace through faith, which means that we rest with faith in the grace that Jesus Christ displayed on the cross (Ephesians 2:9). We cannot save ourselves from our brokenness or do any amount of good works to merit God's favor, but we can have faith that what Jesus accomplished in His death, burial, and resurrection was more than enough for our salvation and our eternal delight. When we accept God, we are commanded to die to our self and our sinful desires, and live a life worthy of the calling we've received (Ephesians 4:1). The gospel compels us to be sanctified, and in so doing, we are conformed to the likeness of Christ Himself. This is hope. This is redemption. This is the gospel.

Thank You

for studying God's Word with us